Fear Not, Weep Not

Scriptures of My Life and Others Too

Fear Not, Weep Not

Scriptures of My Life and Others Too

By

Kevin Cain

For Jesus Christ.... my personal savior

PRELUDE

From the age of around eight years old, I knew I wanted to be a writer because I loved both listening to, and telling, stories. My love for books existed for as long as I can remember. Even before kindergarten or before I learned to read, I owned a sizeable collection of children's picture books. My parents and grandparents often read them to me repeatedly. When no one was around to read to me, I still enjoyed the books by admiring the pictures on every page and making up my own stories with them.

During my second-grade year, I wrote my first short story. It was only one page in length, but I felt as proud of it as a grown adult reaching a lifetime goal. The story told of a haunted bus that once carried passengers around town but, after one of the passengers suffered a heart attack, sat abandoned in the woods near the county road. Each night, so the story went, passing motorists told of seeing a light in the woods coming from the back window of the abandoned bus, right next to the seat where the passenger died. This of course was a work of fiction, but ghost stories were my favorite and continue to fascinate me.

Though I hold a strong love for suspenseful stories, and this genre makes up most of my writing, I also have known my entire life that this gift for writing came about not from my own conjuring. I always knew in my heart that it came as a gift from God. At some point in my life, He wanted me to use it as a tool to somehow help others to come to know of Him and His glory. That's where this book comes into play.

Within these pages lies some of my favorite scriptures that have held important meaning in my life. The first section covers the time in my life when I first accepted Christ as my personal savior. The rest of the sections demonstrate how the scriptures I've chosen aided in my growth, or sanctification as we call it, in my relationship with Him. These are only a few of many scriptures I've learned from. I hope this inspires you in some way, dear reader. I do this not for my own glory or to brag of great things I've accomplishes, as I could have accomplished nothing without Him. I do this for His glory and to show just how important He is to me and how important He can be for you.

In Mathew chapter four, verse four, Jesus said "But he answered, "It is written, ""Man shall not live by bread alone, but by every word that comes from the mouth of God."". Even in teaching His disciples concerning daily prayer, He advised them to pray "Give us this day our daily bread." The "bread" being referred to here isn't the edible kind you bake in the oven but rather the Word of God, or "bread" of life. Jesus placed great importance on scripture and using it in our daily life. Reading he scriptures in some form each day allows us to grow in Him, to learn more about Him and improve our spiritual growth. It strengthens our relationship with God and helps us to become better servants for Him. When it comes to reading the Bible daily, I know I don't always come out perfect, but I try to read scripture almost every day as I know that, without it, I learn nothing and come no closer in my relationship to God. But, after forty-four years of life on this earth, I can look back and see many times in my life where scripture applies.

Some of those times I now illustrate in this Bible in hopes that it might inspire you and your life too. I write this not to boast of my own doings or work. Instead, I do those to boast on God and give him the glory. Please enjoy, and may God bless you and be fruitful in your life as well.

If you confess with your mouth "Jesus is Lord," and believe in your heart that God raised him from the dead, you will be saved. For it is with your heart that you believe and are justified, and it is with your mouth that you confess and are saved.

Romans 10:9-10

In the years I spent living in Adamsville, Alabama, in our little community of Shady Grove, from my birth until the time I left to start my young adult years of independence, I remember only a handful of Sundays where my family missed church. My father served as a deacon and Sunday school teacher, eventually becoming head deacon of our church, and my mother also served as a Sunday school teacher. So, most every Sunday found us within the walls of the church building singing praises and hearing the word preached.

Nothing short of a major illness in the family kept us away from the church doors during my childhood. We arrived every Sunday morning promptly thirty to forty-five minutes prior to the start of Sunday school, which started at nine o'clock in the morning. We stayed through to the end of worship service at eleven-thirty A.M. Then, we returned at four-thirty in the afternoon for the evening school and worship service. On Wednesday evenings, we attended faithfully mid-week church supper and prayer meetings. In short, I never missed out on learning about who God was and what his Son, Jesus Christ, did when he walked the earth. I had the advantage of hearing the gospel very early in life and getting a jump start on the learning process about faith and salvation.

My earliest learnings about Jesus Christ came from the nursery school class at the Baptist church in our hometown. Each Sunday, a different volunteer teacher from the congregation joined us tiny tots in the nursery room and read us stories from the children's storybook version of the Bible. They showed up pictures drawn of the artist's conception of the Bible stories, with everything from Adam and Eve (post-fig leaves) to Noah's Ark to Jonah and the whale. But most importantly, they showed drawings of the story of Jesus. After the stories, we sang children's songs inspired by

Bible verses, such as the song "Jesus Loves Me" and "He's Got the Whole World In His Hands." After our mock choir time, they passed out an art or a craft project, such as a coloring page with an image from that day's lesson to fill in with crayon, or a paper construction kit with glue, popsicle sticks, and anything else needed to make puppet figures of the people or story we learned about that day. We made these projects happily to take home to our mammas, and then we retired to our favorite side of the room for the rest of the duration of class: the toy chest.

In my toddler years and early elementary school years, I held no doubt of who Christ was and that I loved him. Heck, we sang the songs of how we loved Him and how He loved us every Sunday morning in that kids' room at the church. How could I not know? Then came the Sunday when a strange thing happened during the morning worship service, My older brother, at the time in his pre-teen years, got to be baptized by the pastor in that funny little fancy bathtub that rested within these decorative columns in the front of the sanctuary above where the choir sang, and the preacher then preached his sermon.

I remember asking once as a very tiny kid why this awesome tub with glass siding stood in the front of our church high above, and why people bathed in it sometimes during Sunday morning service. Even the preacher joined them in their frolic. Also, why did they only bathe for just a few seconds and while wearing those strange white robes? At home, I was required to bathe for several minutes every night in our tub, and without a stitch of my clothes on. Why couldn't I wear one of those fancy robes when I bathed? It also seemed very strange that these people were willing to bathe in it while the pastor dipped them in front of the whole church. My mother explained though that this strange ritual was not a bath, but rather something called baptism. She went on to say that they did this to show people their dedication to the Christ man I'd learned about for so many years. I asked her when it might be my turn to go play in that church tub. Her answer came as a surprise: it was up to me.

That was easy, I thought. Well then, I want to go let the pastor dunk me in the water next Sunday, I told her. She replied with a smile that this bath was special and took more than just wanting to get in the water. It took making a special dedication for my life. So, for now I was not ready for that church bath. This started sounding stranger to me.

Eventually, my older brother received a turn to go to this baptismal tub to be dunked. I asked my parents how the church came to decide to dunk him, and she said it happened because he asked

Jesus into his heart. Boy, this got stranger and stranger. Did Jesus literally physically shrink and climb into people's hearts? Was he a superhero? No, my mom replied, he's much more than some superhero. Not more than a year later, my sister in turn took a dip into the baptismal one Sunday morning. Now, I really felt left out. How did I go about asking Jesus into my heart if I could not even see him? How did they do that?

The next thing about church that started me questioning was the weird little "supper" they did one a month during our evening service. This took place at the end of the service when the pastor finished preaching. The leading men of our church, the deacons, got up with these gold-colored plates, went down the aisles and passed the plates around. On one plate, sitting within a series of metal holders appeared what looked to me like tiny plastic bathroom cups of grape juice. On the other plates rested a mound of the tiny flat white things that looked like those little square gum candies I often found in gumball machines. The place where my dad took me to get my haircuts had one of those machines. I remembered those white candy tables turned into gum when you chewed them and tasted like mint on the tongue.

But, why were they passing out gum and grape juice to the church congregation? I asked my mom about this strange practice. Another smile crossed her face and she clarified for me that the little white tablets were in fact pieces of bread, and they along with the tiny glasses of juice were to represent the Lord's supper. That's what the final supper Jesus are with his disciples became known as. He broke the bread and blessed it, saying it was like his body given out to us. Then, he took a glass of red wine, blessed it saying it represented his blood poured out for us. He then allowed his disciples to eat of the bread and drink of the wine. My mom explained that our Lord's supper at the church commemorated this even so as to remind us of its importance and what Christ gave for us.

When these plates of bread and juice came passing down my aisle, I noticed that I was never allowed to take from either of them. I wondered what those little tablets tasted like. Would it taste like the bread used for my peanut butter and y sandwiches? Or maybe like those buttery dinner rolls my mom made to go with our dinners. Unfortunately, I was not allowed to find out as, when I reached for the plate, my mother pulled my hand away and advised me not to as it was not time for me to share in the Lord's supper. Now, I really felt confused.

The same explanation sounded from my mother: you are not ready for this. The Lord's supper, she explained, could only be shared with those who asked Jesus into their hearts, or in other words, those who have been "saved." Saved? What did this word mean? Like, rescued from falling off a cliff? Saved from what exactly?

For the next several weeks, I questioned both of my parents occasionally on this idea of being saved. What did it mean and how did I go about being a "saved" person? The answer sounded too simple: just asked Jesus to come into your heart. Surely it could not be that easy. Something so important as to get a dipping into the church's baptismal in front of everybody and gain the right to partake in the tiny wafers and cups of juice must require more than a simple question as that. So came my next question: how do I ask him into my heart? Do I ask out loud? How do I ask if I can't see him? And didn't I already know him anyway from learning about Him in my Sunday School classes and singing songs about my love to Him? What was the difference in that and asking him into my heart? My parents saw my obvious confusions and understood my need for an explanation best suitable for a child my age, which at the time happened to be age twelve.

Our pastor at the time, a great guy we called Brother Batson, was probably the best church pastor I'd ever known. He possessed a wonderful sense of humor, a charming personality and made everyone feel very comfortable and laid back in coming to talk to him about whatever might prey on their hearts and minds. My parents set up a meeting for me in his office one Sunday afternoon prior to the evening church classes. As nice and laid back as I knew him to be, I still felt a bit nervous. My dad was a well-known deacon. Both of my parents were Sunday school teachers in the youth department and known by everyone as strong Christ followers. I felt I needed to be on my best game, to answer every question elegantly that might be thrown my way and sound as smart as possible. Being the immature human being that I was, little did I know I had the idea all wrong.

The Sunday evening of our meeting, I walked into Brother Batson's office at church feeling pretty confidant but just a bit nervous. My parents brought me an hour before the bible group classes were to begin so as to give enough time for our little chat. Brother Batson's blue eyes sparkled as he smiled at me. I always saw him as my favorite pastor ever, at least in my childhood. He loved making us kids laugh and even held a special short children's gathering during every regular worship service on Sunday morning so he could speak to us on our level about the sermon for that day. He also regularly visited the kids in the Christian elementary school held in our church during the week and spoke to them.

He beckoned me to close the door and join him in the guest chair sitting next to him behind his desk. I walked around and sat down, then I noticed a sheet of blank paper lying on his desk in front of him.

"Your parents said you have some questions about how to have a relationship with God," he spoke in his gentle voice.

"I don't understand what that means," I answered him innocently. "I thought I already had a relationship with God by coming to church, reading the Bible and singing songs about him."

He smiled and shook his head. "It's wonderful to do those things because they show obedience to Him. But, it's not the same as having a relationship with Him. It's not quite enough."

Brother Batson took up his black marker and began drawing on his blank paper. He drew a cliff edge on each side. On top of the left cliff, he drew a small stick figure to represent me. On the right cliff, he drew a large stick figure to represent God. In the middle of the page between the cliffs, he left a blank abyss.

"This represents you and God," he said. You want to join God, yes?"

I shook my head in agreement.

"Now," he continued, "what happens if you try walking out from that cliff all on your own to reach God?" He then drew a line from the cliff that suddenly dropped into the abyss. "You can't. At least, not on your own."

He drew a cross in the abyss directly between the cliff edges and wrote the name Jesus within the cross. Above the cross, he drew a dotted path from one cliff edge to the other.

Brother Batson looked back at me with a smile. "In order to reach God, your need Jesus as your savior to stop you from dropping into the abyss of sin. How do you suppose you do that?"

I shrugged my shoulders.

"First, you need to be sure that you want Him to be your savior for life."

"I do," I answered rather quickly.

"Good, then. Next, you have to go to him prayerfully and privately. Tell Him that you place all your trust in Him. You give all of your heart and soul to him. Ask Him to forgive you for your sins, and mean it with all of your heart. Let Him know that you believe He is the one true Savior and the only thing you need for salvation. Tell Him that you give your life to Him and ask Him to lead you always."

I looked at my pastor in astonishment. "That's it? It's that easy?"

"Well," he chuckled, "it may sound easy, but you have to really mean it. You have to spend the rest of your life trusting in Him, keeping your faith alive that He is enough to save you. You must love always, ask for daily forgiveness, pray to Him regularly and lay all of your worries and troubles at his feet. And, you must keep your trust and faith alive that He will always come through in some way."

As he spoke these words to me, I felt a warmth grow in my heart. I felt a "tugging" at my heart, which is the best way I can describe it. As if something were pulling at my soul urgently. The memories of Sunday school classes gone by in my earlier childhood flashed through my mind. Images of me coloring in images of Christ coming from his tomb that the teacher passed out in nursery class when I was five, or of the neat paper puppets we made of Him descending vertically across a sheet of art paper into paper clouds. The songs we sang in children's choir of how He loves us and we love Him.

Was all of this teaching me and leading me up to an even more important decision in my life?

The wonderful thing about learning so young about Christ and what he did to forgive our sins made it so much easier for me to make this decision. For me, no other decision even existed other than a big fat YES. Later that week during one of my prayer times, I quietly asked Christ to forgive me of my sins, come into my heart and my soul. I told him that from then on, I trust Him to be in control of my life and to be my ultimate Savior for the rest of time. My thinking at the time may not have been mature enough to understand the utmost importance of what I was asking, but I understood why I needed to ask, and that the decision was not one to be put off any longer. I needed His forgiveness and to trust Him as my Savior for the salvation needed and the link to having any kind of relationship with God.

I happily told my parents of my prayer immediately after. The following week, during the altar call at the end of the Sunday morning service, I approached our pastor and informed him of my prayer and decision to trust in Christ to be part of my life and my savior. He took my hands and shook them in both of his, congratulating me. We went about planning my baptism.

Two weeks later, I stepped out into the baptismal pool in the front of our sanctuary above the robed choir and allowed Brother Batson to dunk me in the water in the name of the Father, the Son and the Holy Spirit. This was, still is and always will be the best bath I ever took. My family, including my grandparents from both sides, sat in the front pews watching as I was dipped back into that cool water and brought up a changed person. At least, changed on the inside.

From that day of my prayer to Christ dedicating my life to Him until now, I never regretted my decision. I never once looked back to wonder if the decision I made mattered at all. I know it did. The proof of that lies in the fact that, through my life growing up, through school, college, work and adulthood, I never wanted for anything. He always has provided everything I need, and He always will. I've never been without a roof over my head. I've never gone hungry. There have always been clothes on my back and shoes on my feet, and a warm bed for me to sleep in. But, even without all of those material things, I know I'd still trust in Christ as my savior. I trust in God the Father to be in control of all things. I believe fully that he gave us His son Jesus as a sacrifice so that, through the Son, we have a path to God for forgiveness and sanctification.

John 3:16 says "For God so loved the world that he gave his only begotten son, and whosoever believeth in him shall not perish but have eternal life." Over the years, I've heard some people, even pastors, attempt to add a sort of "fine print" to this statement by saying "But you also have to do this" and "But if you're not doing that, then no," BUT, this scripture holds no fine print. It says "whoever believeth in him," and that is all it takes for the salvation. We must fully believeth in Him to the point of having a relationship with Him in our daily lives, but there is no fine print to it. We cannot "earn" our way into it by good works or going to church every time the doors open. It takes Jesus and Jesus alone to save us.

Am I perfect now because of accepting Him as my savior? In human terms, certainly not. I still sin, stumble and fall short, but I have Jesus to turn to for daily forgiveness and to pick me back up to continue down the path of life. Just like the poem about the two sets of footprints in the sand becoming one, He is there to carry me through my life's trials, so I possess no fear for what lies in the future. How wonderful it feels to live without fear or worry overwhelming me. How wonderful it is to have a Savior to turn to in my darkest times, to talk to in prayer about my innermost pains. I no longer fear things like death or waking up tomorrow. I do no fear Satan and temptation, as I know that, no matter what happens, Jesus holds my soul within himself, and no devil or demon can ever separate it. My faith in Him will remain alive until the end.

God is our refuge and strength, a very present help in trouble. Therefore we will not fear though the earth gives way, though the mountains be moved into the heart of the sea, though its waters roar and foam, though the mountains tremble at its swelling.

Psalm 46: 1-3

The neighborhood of Shady Acres, the place of my childhood from birth through college, lies hidden very deeply in the forests and hills of the western part of Jefferson County in central Alabama. So far out do the winding county roads lead to it that visitors to our house in the times before GPS almost gave up to being lost in the woods before they found it. The woods encircled our neighborhood and ran right behind my house at the edge of our back yard. We lived on less than an acre of property, so the woods rested only steps away from the back of the house. A hillside sloped down from the edge of our back yard to a pipeline about a football field's distance away. The pipeline created a clearing that we called the "holler" below our property. Many thick clusters of pine and oak trees dotted the hillside between our property and that line.

As children often do, we told many ghost stories about those thick, dark woods. During the daylight, the trees let in just enough sunlight to dust a bit of the forest floor with its glow. At night, it grew the darkest pitch of black and looked menacing. So, in our creative minds, we conjured up all kinds of ghosts and creatures living out there amongst the shadow. One outlandish story involved a lizard man who lived in the pipe that ran under the entry street to our neighborhood where the pipeline ran. Stream water normally ran through it after heavy rains, and some of the kids attempted to say the pitter-patter noises we heard below the street there were the sounds of the lizard man moving around. Most likely, those noises were only moisture dripping from the roof of the pipe and the trickling of the rainwater moving through, but what an exciting story the lizard man made.

Many a time came when a friend of mine dared me or each other to go into those woods. "If you don't last more than five minutes in there without running back out, you're a loser," was an example of the many taunts I heard amongst friends in the neighborhood. I do admit that standing in the middle of those woods always made me feel like someone or something was watching me from the trees. The wind blowing through sounded like whispered voices of ghosts, the crunching of the leaves nearby like some creature getting ready to pounce. Of course, all of these things had logical explanations to them, but not always to the mind of a scared child.

The fear of the dark tormented me about like most children ever feel tortured by it. Although I never experienced any problems sleeping, I spent some waking moments prior to drifting off into slumberland just thinking about what terrors might be hiding within those shadows sprouting up from the corners of my bedroom. This led to some reoccurring dreams I experienced between the ages of four and five. The dreams consisted of this wicked old woman who looked like the traditional which from fairy tales and television. She wore a long, flowing black dress with a closed collar and ruffled sleeves. Her straggly black hair hung down on her shoulders and framed her pasty face. Her flesh on her face and hands always appeared so ghastly white, looking as if someone had just thrown baby powder on her.

When she appeared to me, she always held up her hands and cackled. Her fingers displayed these long, curling, pitch black fingernails that ended in points so sharp they looked as if they possessed the ability to pierce bone. In several of these dreams, she appeared from my closet in the darkness as I tried to sleep under the covers. Her face glowed with this eerily green color like glow-in-the-dark silly putty smeared on someone's flesh. In other dreams, she came out of the dark woods behind our house. Sometimes, the dream might even be a pleasant one where I was simply shopping in the grocery story with my mother, and this evil woman would pop out unsuspectedly from one of the aisles, her hands raised, her fingernails displayed and the same cackle escaping her cracked lips.

She always snagged my clothes with those long nails and carried me away from my screaming mother. In the dreams with the closet, she rushed out toward my bed, threw back the foot of my covers and latched those nails onto my ankles. She then proceeded to drag toward the dark, yawning abyss of my bedroom closet doorway. I always clawed at the carpet and screamed for my parents, both to no avail. Every time, she successfully dragged me through that closet door, and the door slammed, leaving me screaming in darkness, each time waking up at that moment thrashing in the covers of my bed. The funny thing is that I never felt terrified of my closet in my waking hours or even going into it to play. It only appeared menacing in those dreams.

What awful images to plague a five-year-old child's subconscious! I don't know what caused such horrid dreams other then my fear of the darkness while drifting off to sleep. Nothing dark existed in my life, at least at that time of my life, so that fear could only be the prompting factor.

When I think of fear and the Bible, I remember the story of David. One in particular that most all kids who ever attended church have heard is the telling of the time David faced a creature of his own. David was the youngest son of a man named Jesse, a farmer and sheep breeder who lived amongst the Israelite tribe. A day came when David found himself suddenly brought out of the fields by the summoning of a man named

Samuel who professed to be a prophet and saw great things in store for this young man. Before long, David found himself working as the aide to King Saul, and then himself becoming King. However, in his early days he proved beyond doubt that trust in God beats the fear of anything and in any place.

David and his family lived in the nation of Israel. A nearby nation of tough bullies called the Philistines challenged the Israelites to war. Saul, the king of Israel, sent his troops to meet the Philistines in a valley, and there each nation line up on opposite sides of the valley. To the horror of the Israelites and their king, the Philistines sent forward their largest warrior, a giant by the name of Goliath. He stood at nine feet in height, was very broad and possessed muscular arms and legs that were each as big around as a normal man's full body. The Israelites and Saul backed away.

David's brothers were all called into the army to fight this battle. David however found himself rejected because of his small stature. After all, the army wanted the toughest looking warriors they could find, especially standing up to such large bullies as the Philistines. But when they all beheld the size of Goliath the Giant, what fear each of them must have felt in the moment. What trembling their bodies must have experienced. And, what surprise must have overcome them when, of all people, tiny little David, the same one they felt too small for the job before, stepped forward and offered to battle this gigantic man. When Goliath saw this tiny boy walk onto the field offering to fight, he laughed.

Remember the bullies in school? The ones larger than you than made you panic just by walking through the same school hallway as you? You dared not stand in their way or even make eye contact with them for fear of being beaten up. This most likely is exactly how the Israelites felt. David, in his small stature, could have easily allowed himself to feel that same terror. However, he chose not to.

Why did David choose not to fear? Because he knew God's strength. He felt God's calling to step forward and not let fear control him. Instead of fleeing to the nearest cave and hiding within until the dust settled outside, he instead chose a rock from the ground to use in the simple sling he brought with him. Not a sword or shield or other such large weapon. A simple slingshot. He loaded the rock into the sling, reared back and hurled it at the might forehead of the laughing giant. David knew without a shadow of doubt that God would use that rock to stop the enemy, regardless of how weak that he himself might be. The rock sailed through the air, hit Goliath in the forehead and sent him plummeting to the ground in eternal silence. Shocked by their mightiest warrior being slain by this tiny fellow, the rest of the Philistines ran in terror. Isn't that an amazing thought? The bullies who showed up to the fight fully confident that they'd send their tiny adversaries fleeing in terror were, instead, fleeing in terror themselves.

The difference made here lies within the simple faith David held for God to protect him and help him overcome this giant hurdle of fear. I firmly believe that when he stepped out onto that field, he knew in his heart that God's protection surrounded him. Though to any average person, stepping out in front of a giant and then using a rock to try to kill him without getting stomped sounds a bit far-fetcher. Perhaps even David had temporary doubts about this feat, but he still stepped out there. I believe he felt God in his heart telling him that it was okay. David lay his fear on God to take over, and He gave David the confidence needed to step forward. Then, David used the talent he had with him at the time, his slingshot, and let God work through him. This is why the rock hurled through the air and into the forehead of the massive Goliath did the job so perfectly. God led it to do so, and David's faith in God to work through him paid off.

How did this apply to my life? It reminds me of the many scriptures in the Bible where God asks us to lay down our heavy burdens, our worries, our fears, and let Him take them. As the title scripture of this chapter tells us not to fear no matter what the earth, the universe around us or life itself throws our way, each time I become afraid of something, I remind myself of God's protection.

As I grew from a small toddler into a young boy and gained more knowledge about God, I learned even then to turn to Him for protection whenever I awoke from a nightmare or faced something that looked scary to me. I prayed each night before bedtime for Jesus's protection and for his angels to watch over me and our household. With that, the nightmares of the cackling woman in the closet desisted.

When I feared an upcoming test of class project at school, I prayed for my fear to be taken away and for Him to help me with the knowledge I needed to pass. Or if I feared some teacher giving me a hard time, I prayed for His protection and also prayed for Him to work on the teacher's heart and attitude.

When I feared someone bullying me, I prayed for is protection and gave my fears to Him.

When I feared the wrath of my parents when I did something wrong, I prayed for His forgiveness for my wrongdoing, for His protection and gave my fears to Him.

When I feared the night or the darkness in my bedroom, I prayed for His protection and gave my fears to Him.

Becoming an adult does not mean fears are forever removed from your life. It certainly does not mean never facing another nightmare like you did as a child. I faced plenty and still face plenty.

Whenever I fear a tough obstacle at work such as a tough client or a hard file to work, I pray for his protection, the strength and knowledge that I need, and I give my fears to Him.

When I fear because I accidently make a mistake that might be costly, I turn it over to Him for guidance and protection.

When I fear heavy finances for the month, I turn it over to Him and pray for his guidance and protection.

When I fear the dangers of society or traveling, I pray to Him for protection and guidance. I turn my fears to Him to handle.

I trust in Him with every step of my life. When I do, I find that I no longer hold fear in my heart or mind.

You see, we all face our own Goliaths in life. God gave us a stone all of our own to take down those giants, or mountains of fear, in our lives. That stone is our savior Christ Jesus. As Deuteronomy 31:8 puts it, "The Lord himself goes before you and will be with you; he will never leave you nor forsake you. Do not be afraid; do not be discouraged." Nothing protects us better than Him. Of that, I am completely convinced.

Next time a giant stands up in our life or a nightmare threatens your peace, why not turn to God and ask Him to load up your slingshot? I can guarantee you have nothing to lose.

He gives strength to the weary and increases the power of the weak. Even youths grow tired and weary, and young men stumble and fall; but those who hope in the Lord will renew their strength. They will soar on wings like eagles; they will run and not grow weary, they will walk and not be faint.

Isaiah 40: 29-31

On days during the seasons with moderate temperatures, like spring and late fall when the Alabama outdoor air feels less like a blast from a furnace, my mom loved to take walks for her exercise. In the afternoon after returning home from work but before supper, she liked to go out and walk a mile, sometimes even a few miles, down our neighborhood roads and even into the neighborhood across the holler from ours. She walked until the skin of her forehead turned the shade of a ripened tomato and beads of sweet turned into streams drifting down her face.

I often wondered, being the young and uneducated child that I was, why she chose to walk such long distances. Surely her feet must have throbbed after every journey. They certainly showed signs of blisters and peeling skin on her toes whenever she collapsed barefooted on the couch in her nightgown after a warm shower. What caused me to cringe even more though were the times she requested us kids and my dad to join her. There never failed to sound a groan or three whenever she made this request.

My mother, never the fool when it came to dealing with her kids, always knew the way to get us motivated to join her. The motivation: she promised us ice cream from the nearby Shady Grove Sandwich Shop on the way back from our walk. The sandwich shop sat in a tiny strip of shops on the main road and near the entrance road into our neighborhood. The woman who ran the store along with her husband always held a good supply of homemade chocolate and vanilla ice cream. This cream tasted completely different from that found in the freezer sections of grocery stores. This stuff tasted fresh from the churn. The chocolate always remained my favorite as, not only did we get generous portions in our large waffle cones, but the lady of the store always left a large chocolate malt ball at the bottom of the cone beneath the ice cream like a treasure awaiting our mouths to dig it out.

The offer of ice cream always lightened the otherwise foreboding prospect of walking miles down the road and back in the Alabama heat. So, with our complaining subdued, we slapped our sneakers to our feet and hit the door.

Another added bonus to these walks was the view of the nature alongside the road. Alabama is famous for its kudzu growth. Mainly found in Asia, this plant works like a mold in that it continuously grows and spreads. It creates a nuisance when found in one's yard or alongside one's house, but out in the wild of nature, it does present a beautiful touch to the scenery when hanging from the tree limbs or wrapped around the bottom of the large trunk of an oak. Another type of plant we often saw were elephant ear plants, called that because of their largeness and the shape resembling that of an elephant's ear, of course. We saw many of these growing at the edge of the woods along with the shrubs near the shoulders of our neighborhood road.

We strode the long walk down the main road of our neighborhood, exited the entrance where the Sandwich Shop and its heavenly ice cream awaited us, and strolled into the next neighborhood known as Indian Meadows. The name for this community came from the history of the land belonging to the Cherokee Native Americans hundreds of years ago. We often found arrowheads and broken pottery, remnants left from the days of those Native Americans, in the soil of our woods when we explored. Not only did the area possess Native American History, but it also possessed an old cemetery located right behind the houses of the neighborhood. The cemetery dated all the way back to the early 1800's and the early settlers of that area.

Whenever we walked past that old cemetery, I always failed to keep my curiosity in check and stole a glance over to it. The cemetery sat back behind the houses there, and the houses had a good fifty-to-sixty foot distance from their fronts to the street shoulder. But, as we walked past the houses, a glance to the spaces between them revealed the tombstones in the cemetery beyond their back yards. Rumor had it that some of the back yards had unmarked graves, and some of those unmarked graves even rested in the ground directly underneath the homes. This led to many ghost stories and legends about the area* that floated amongst the kids and teenagers as they attempted to scare each other. And of course, it in turn gave me the willies each time we walked or even drove past in that neighborhood.

"Just don't look over there. Face forward and keep walking straight ahead," my mom always responded when she saw how silly we looked with our scared expression. "Nothing over there's going to bother you. Those people aren't even there, just their bodies. Their spirits have gone to be with God."

The fear was easily overcome as we got on past the graveyard. The hardest obstacle, the part not so easy to overcome, came with the exhaustion of the walk. Onward we pressed in our walk-a-thon. Cars passed us by on the main street. Some drivers gave us a glance with an expression of wonder as to what these folks were doing walking on the side of the road. Others recognized our family and gave a honk for greeting as they passed, which my mother returned with a quick but friendly wave of her hand without breaking any part of her stride. By the time we reached

*See my book "The Legends of Indian Narrows: Ghostly Childhood Memoirs"

the point of the road where we normally turned around to head back, we kids were panting, leaning forward as we walked, stumbling and eventually collapsing off the grassy side of the road. Mom somehow possessed this explosive everlasting energy when it came to walking. Nothing seemed to tire her. No amount of sweat beading her sun-reddened forehead took away any energy from her stride. She turned to look down at us and put her hands on her hips, shaking her head.

"Come on, guys. It's not that bad. You can do it. We didn't really walk as far as you think. The tiredness is all just in your mind."

"Are you kidding," I screamed, wiping the sweat from my forehead and dusting loose grass blades from my socks. "It's hot and I'm dying! Somebody go back and get the car for us!"

She laughed and shook her head. "No, you aren't. You can do it. You need to just make up your mind that you can do it and nothing is going to stop you." I'm sure that she viewed us through the eyes of a mother, she knew her babies and that we did not look nearly as exhausted as we put on to be, and she proved right. "Just rest a minute and then we will continue, but you and all of us will walk home together. That is, after we get some ice cream for you on the way back. If you can get up for that."

The ice cream trick won again. We stood and dusted our legs off after a few moments. Then, we turned back in the direction we came and began our march homeward. Contrary to my belief that death loomed large before us, we did reach the ice cream shop safe and sound, enjoyed our treat, and then we did reach home safely to shower and relax without the grim reaper knocking at our door.

I tell this story as it continues to be my earliest memory of a time I felt like a task at hand or journey before me seemed way to difficult to handle. Many times, I found myself faced with obstacles I felt that, surely, I'd never overcome. Some of them even felt like the end of the world.

What my mother taught me with those walks was, no matter how difficult an obstacle may seem, you cannot let your worry of failure or growing weary stop you from proceeding on with what you need to do. We needed those walks to keep us healthy, to get us out of the house and active in the outdoors more often. I saw those walks as trial and tribulation, where the road seemed to keep stretching on and the journey made me feel like no end existed in sight, though deep inside I knew better. What

I needed to remember was to keep strong, keep pushing forward and, in the end, a wonderful prize awaited as promised!

In the same way, God knows what is best for us and our lives. He knows the very destiny of our outcomes before we are even born. Instead of worrying about how hard a struggle might be, why not instead ask God for his strength and wisdom to get through the struggle? Why not trust in him that, now matter how bad that struggle looks, beyond it will come a positive outcome as long as we trust in God to get us there? Why not let Him take the lead, push forward on and trust that He will get us to the end successfully?

In another early example where I witnessed God's leadership in a situation I thought would surely lead to disaster, I once worked at a local department store which, for the sake of security, I will only call "The Big Store." I started working at said store straight out of high school during the late nineteen-nineties so as to afford buying a car, gas and insurance for that car and also to pay my tuition out of pocket for the courses I enrolled in at the local community college. My plan was to work and go to school at the same time, though the hours and amount of work seemed overwhelming. Still, I trusted in God to see me through it on both my work and my studies.

My plan once I got through the first two years of college at the community college level was to first complete the academic course requires, then transfer to the nearby four-year college where I could focus more on my major studies. I went to school mostly in the day and worked evenings until late at night at the Big Store where I worked as a cashier and then a salesfloor associate. Because of the mess that customers made in just about every aisle of the store, the management made us employees, including cashiers, stay very late at night after closing cleaning up the aisles and straightening the merchandise on all of the shelves from one end of the entire salesfloor to the other. The store was humongous, so it often took us two or three hours after the eleven o'clock closing time to get our tasks completed. Once, it took us until three o'clock the following morning to complete it and leave. You'd be shocked too at what garbage some of the customers left behind, such as chewed gum, dirty food wrappers, large paper cups full of soda, and even cups with chewed tobacco spittle in them left up behind our merchandise on the back of the shelf where some dirty man obviously shoved it once he was done spitting his chaw.

I washed my hands at least a dozen times before the night was through. By the time we finished, the small group of us stumbled out the exit doors into the blackness of the night and the parking lot where we prayed no muggers lay in wait. As employees we were required to park in the farthest section of the lot so customers would have spaces available closer to the store. Never mind we had to risk our lives because this business offered no type of security protection other than one lone manager standing at the entrance door watching us walk to our cars.

Since I went to my college classes early in the morning, with the earliest starting at eight o' clock, it took quite a struggle to stay awake and keep paying attention to my teachers and their lessons. God help me whenever I had quizzes or tests as those came much harder than they should to pass due to my exhaustive time at work the late night before. But, did our management at the store care about us college students (believe me, I was not the only student working there) and the lateness we worked? Of course not.

I made my concerns about these later hours known to our head store manager. He walked back to the warehouse with me to talk in private. He let me know that, going forward, he would ask his assistant managers to allow me and any college student to leave after an hour from the store closing if clean up was not completed by that time. He assured me the assistant managers would know that evening. I went out to the salesfloor and return to my work satisfied in making my concern know and appreciating it being heard.

For a week, this order from the head manager worked out. The assistant managers who stayed late to close the store made sure to get us kids out no more than an hour after closing. I went home to get a good rest and made it to the college on time the next morning. My relief came short-lived however when the next Sunday evening rolled around. The assistant manager in charge of closing that evening kept us past the one hour mark after closing. I let it go for another hour, continuing to work with the rest of the remaining employees to straighten up shelves around the store.

After a few hours past, I went to the assistant manager and asked about leaving. She looked confusedly at her watch and told me that we still had a while to go before anyone would be allowed to leave. I explained the situation and the order from the head manager for college kids to leave no later than one hour past closing. She shrugged and said she knew nothing of this and I needed to get back to work and then we might get out in just a little while. I felt great annoyance at this but went on about my work until we left about thirty minutes later.

The next time I returned to work that week, I went with my department manager into the back of the store. We went into the head manger's office to discuss what had occurred. The sudden change in the store manager reminded me of the transformation scene in *Dr. Jekyll and Mr. Hyde* when he drinks the potion to start the metamorphosis. The manager's face went from pleasant to crinkled and angry in just a few seconds. Do you supposed he was angry at the manager not adhering to his order? If so, you'd be wrong. His anger instead came in my direction!

"Look here," he preached through gritted teeth, "I'm running a business here! We need this store straightened every evening by everyone who is working that night. And, if that means you have to stay here late to help make me look good, I don't care if you have classes the very next morning, you have to stay here and help make me look ***GOOD***!"

The voice of thought in my mind whispered quietly to myself, "I don't think there's anybody on this earth who can help make him look good because he is ***UUUUGLY***! I struggled to keep the laughter inside. But, another huge part of me felt the icy realization that this man, who seemed to care about his employees before, gave no thought or care to our predicament. We were indeed being used like slaves and peons to help make him look great to his higher-ups without him so much as lifting his pinky-finger to help. We college students were on our own to continue suffering in body, in soul, in mind and in our educational at the hands of these slavedrivers. Needless to say, we felt trapped.

From that day going forward while I worked there, he and the rest of management treated me like one of the worst employees they ever had. Though I worked my entire shift to get my own department straightened and cleaned before closing so that I could go into the other departments to help them once we closed (mind you, I worked the department and register where highly expensive electronics were kept and sold, and I was not allowed per the store's security policy to leave that department for any reason other than for lunch, where another employee would spell me, or to make a quick trip to the bathroom). I worked feverishly without any further complaints. I filled their shelves and aisle showcases with stock each time items ran out. And yet, the assistant manager over our area of the store acted as if I were a lazy person who had to constantly be pushed to work.

On my off days where I went to classes only, I tried seeking out employment elsewhere at other stores and local banks. One of the places I sought out employment happened to be my own credit union. I applied for the of bank teller, and shortly after I received an invite for an interview. When I showed up, I sat as requested by the receptionist in a waiting room alone and waited. My arrival time, as I normally do for interviews, was ten minutes before my appointed time. However, the interviewer kept me waiting at least twenty minutes past the time of our appointment.

When she finally came out, she had three girls on either side of her and led them out laughing and talking to them. She said, "Girls, let me take you to your new bosses!" so happily with the widest grin on her face. She stole a glimpse my way but continued on without any other acknowledgement my way. When she returned, she leaned down over me in my chair, the smile completely vanished and her eyes narrowed as if skeptically sizing me up. She said to me, "Excuse me, are you here for something? Can I help you? What are you doing here?"

I felt completely shocked at this "welcome," if you'd call it that, from her as I had an appointment scheduled with her, and that appointment was made several days in advance. I thought she should at least know she had an interview scheduled. Trying to stay as polite and professional as I could, I responded, "Hello. My name is Kevin Cain, and we had an appointment scheduled for eleven o'clock this morning. I made sure to arrive early but they asked me to just wait here."

She still sized me up with her narrow gaze, shrugged and said, "Well, wait here until I come back with the test. We have a test we require every applicant to complete before we interview them."

I assumed this test might be like some others that I've taken at interviews that contain psychological questions or perhaps questions to analyze skills in certain areas. I waited confidently until she came back with the one-page test, handed it to me with a pencil and asked me to sit at the nearby table and take it, requesting me to just bring it on into her office when I finished. I sat down with the paper and scanned it. The test was nothing but extremely easy elementary school math problems like "what does two plus two equal?" I completed it in several seconds and, confused as to why such a ridiculous test might be given, talked it back into her office.

She snatched the test from my hand, looked it over, scowled as if disappointed I did not miss any of the answers, and proceeded with the interview where she interrogated me harshly. I wondered the whole time if perhaps she might have like me more had I been a girl. I won't go into any further detail here as it is beside the point, and, needless to say, I did not get the job at this credit union. I tell this story only to describe how dejected I felt trying to find another job, and some of the harshness I ran into while searching. I felt like giving up, like I'd never find that great job.

However, even through these trials, I refused to let my faith down. I prayed to God to lead me, to keep me from giving up, to strengthen me and help me find that job. I only knew I had to get out of Big Store before I lost my sanity completely! And I prayed for same profusely!

I continued my job at Big Store for a while longer. Eventually, the nephew of one of our managers found himself hired and placed in the same department where I worked. At first he seemed friendly enough, but a short amount of time revealed just how lazy he was. We worked evenings, and often he wandered out of the department while I continued to help customers with products. Sometimes he wandered to other departments where he carried on conversations with other employees, and sometimes he drifted off to the back warehouse where other employees reported to me that he hung around playing with toys and goofing off. When a manger walked by, he suddenly showed up with a stack of merchandise and busied himself stocking shelves. But, once the managers turned their sights elsewhere, he returned to his lazy, casual behavior.

The time came when I transferred from my community college to the four-year college in the city. I finally received approval for financial aid which took the burden of paying the tuition out-of-pocket off of my back. As time went on and I took more full-time classes at the four-year college to try to work through my major, I felt more and more pressure at work from management and dealing with the rude public at large which effected my studies and grades, not to mention what little sleep I got. I debated throwing in the towel completely on the job side. It seemed out of the question to do such a thing because I needed my paycheck. At the time, I was still living at home traveling from the outskirts of the county to school and back, plus traveling to work and back, and I needed gas money. I needed money for food and my share of expenses at home as well.

One night after once again being chastised by a manager, I went into the last aisle of my department where no customers were around. I went to the middle of the aisle and, facing the shelves, I dropped to my knees and prayed to God for strength and to tell me what to do.

"Go.....home," a voice whispered in my ear.

No way, I thought to myself. I can't just leave. As much as I hate it here, I need my paycheck.

"Go.....home," the voice said again.

I can't, my brain responded. How will I pay for my gas? My vehicle maintenance and insurance? The other things I need?"

"Go....home," the voice insisted.

In my heart, I felt the overwhelming sense and peace of mind that the time came to leave this job behind regardless. Right now. I would be cared for and need not worry. God had something better for me in store.

I stood up from the cold cement floor of that store aisle, dusted the knees of my pants legs off and turned to find my coworker turning the corner into the aisle. She looked at me in wonder.

"I can't do this anymore. I'm sorry," I said to her and then left the aisle. I walked out of the department and straight down the main aisle toward the back of the store. I went through the swinging doors into the stock room, through the back hall and into the manager's office where I took of my smock and employee badge, folded the smock and laid it on the manager's desk with my badge on top. Turning quickly without another thought, I left the office, walked out of the stock room, straight through the store in a brisk walk and exited the front doors. It was the first and only time in my life that I ever walked off a job.

Before I describe the day outside, I must mention that, when I traveled to work earlier that day, a heavy rain fell and storms with lightning sent thunderous shivers around the area. The local weatherman even came over the television reporting of possible severe weather with tornado watches. When I entered the store earlier, the rain continued to pound the asphalt of the parking lot outside. Now, as I exited the front door of that store, leaving that terrible job behind, I stepped out into beautiful sunshine. The rain had ceased, and the clouds parted, and that sun shined down brightly, sparking on the rooftops of the cars parked outside.

I took a breath of the fresh air and exhaled, feeling a lot of weight of burden suddenly release from my mind and soul. It felt so invigorating experiencing that freedom. No more would I be required to put up with cleaning up dirty shelves, being held prisoner until all hours of the night and early morning, and not dealing with scummy, backstabbing store managers. I drove home feeling elated but at the same time saddened and worried over how my parents would probably respond.

When I got home and told them, I broke down and released my emotions through tears. My mom took me in her arms and held me a while as I cried. My dad picked up the phone, called my ex-store manager and told him what he thought of him and what a hardworking employee that he and his store had just lost. The manger just sighed and responded with, "Well, he never really gave us a change to get to know him." How ridiculous that response sounded. After all, I'd given them three years of my life in that store.

Six months crept by as I continued searching for new work. Meanwhile, my schoolwork improved greatly, and so did my self-esteem and confidence. From the time I walked off the job until starting the next, I had just enough money to get by on, as coincidence would have it. Perhaps not coincidence, but God looking out for me.

After six months, a position came open at my university for a worker in the bookstore. The pay was more than I paid per hour at Big Store, and the management so much better and nicer. I started work there immediately and began earning my keep once again. The most awesome part of that job was the ability to work and go to school at the same location. When time for classes came around, all I had to do was clock out and walk over to the student class buildings. Afterwards, I could return to work.

"Your schoolwork and education come first," my wonderful new boss exclaimed. He was the first manager to treat me not only like a hardworking employee but also like a son. He treated us all very well and looked after us. Yes, indeed, this job was a definite Godsend!

Several different people from different backgrounds worked at the bookstore during my tenure there. One in particular was a student there who I will call Evan who worked in the computers area selling computers, software programs and computer accessories to students and teachers alike. Evan started out an atheist. He believed the world and life itself came along from the "big bang" and evolution, nothing more. A friend of mine, who I will call Stella, believed in the same Christian faith as I, and she also happened to be the wife of a pastor. She worked in the school supply department, and we often had Bible study discussions and even prayer together.

Evan stopped by our department almost daily to hear our discussions and chime in on his beliefs. Though he liked to tease us with his "facts," we always remained friendly and held very polite discussions, hearing him out on his opinion completely and then providing our feedback, or counter-discussion as it were. He did listen with attentive ears, and his facial expression and reactions told me that he did take our explanations to heart. As for his talk on the "big bang" and evolution, I always explained back to him that, even if you added those factors in, it all had to start from some higher being. The "big bang" couldn't happen on its own. Something... or someone.... higher had to cause it. This made him think.

When I made mistakes, such as getting angry and saying a swear word under my breath, or doing something else considered a trivial sin, Evan never failed to catch me on that and say "See, you sinned. You call that a relationship with God?"

I always answered with, "Becoming a Christian does not make you perfect nor does it mean you will never, ever stumble across sin again. But, what it does mean is that we have a savior Jesus to take that daily sin to for forgiveness and to wipe the slate clean. I put my faith in Him for forgiveness and I turn from it and worry no further."

After a few years of working together, some of what Stella and I discussed with Evan seemed to rub off. One day, he came into the store and declared to us his decision to start going to church so he could learn more about this God and this savior Jesus we kept talking about. He wanted to study it all further. Several months passed, and Evan announced his decision to accept Christ as his savior.

Shortly after, he was baptized during one of his church's Sunday morning worship services before the congregation, and before long he even became a Sunday School leader. Quite the drastic change from the Evan whom we knew a few years before.

So, what does this have to do with the scripture I began this chapter with and the story from my childhood about suffering through walks with my mom?

I compare this long journey of going through dealing with a nightmare job to those walks from childhood. In both cases, the struggle seemed very real and very tiring. I felt deflated at one point, even considering throwing in the "I'm Done With This" flag, so to speak, and giving up. But, just as my mom assured me when I felt at my most tired and weary in the walk, God assured me in the trials of this horrible job at Big Store that this was only temporary and the weariness only in my mind. I could do this! I could fight my way through the struggle while keeping my faith alive that, in the end, a rich reward awaited. In the case of the walks, ice cream at the Sandwich Shop awaited me. In the case of the horrid job of my young adult years, what awaiting was something much better: a job I would enjoy doing, managers to enjoy working for and with, perfect harmony between the job and my schooling, and even participating in the salvation of a soul otherwise lost.

I know the voice whispering to me that day in the store aisle telling me to go home belonged to God. I strongly feel that true in my heart even to this day. Had I not kept the faith to not quit and then allowed my fear to keep me from listening when He told me it was finally to leave, I might have been stuck in a worse condition. Instead, He came through and I found myself in a much better place. Not only that, but God used me at the same time to help someone else in need of knowing Him. I cannot think of anything else in the universe better than that result!

This struggle came around again in recent years of my career. In the company where I work now, I've worked and fought hard to may myself valuable over the last few decades. Whenever an opportunity for a good promotion comes along, I throw in my hat without hesitation so long as God makes me feel comfortable in proceeding to do so. Sometimes, I get turned down and watch while others who have not been at the company near as long as me sort of leap-frog their way past while I get left waiting longer for my turn. Other times, my perseverance and faith in God pays off and I am allowed into that higher level of employment status. One thing is for sure though...no matter what the outcome, I still keep my faith in God and his leadership alive. No matter how many times life and the world disappoints me, God never will. Because, though the mountains of life seem high and the waves of disappointments come crashing, I truly believe He will continue to be there for me and strengthen me through it as He promised that He would.

It's a hard walk, but endurance in your faith will pay off.

If we confess our sins, he is faithful and just and will forgive us from all unrighteousness

1 John 1:9

Oh, there I went again. I tripped over a temptation. It looked way too inviting. It felt too good. But, in God's word, it falls under (fill in the blank with whatever daily sin you might think of: lust, greed, jealousy, hatred for something or someone). Here I thought I was saved through Christ and never to walk the path of sin. So, why did I just stumble over one and let it make me fall?

Once upon a time, if I'd asked this question to a traditional pastor, chances are I'd get the answer "Well, boy, perhaps you'd best check you relationship with God 'cuz there's something wrong there." Probably not all pastors might give that answer, but guaranteed some jump to that simple conclusion. And doesn't that sound correct? Why, just think about it. If your relationship with God is so solid, why would you fall to a temptation? Or two? Or even three? There can't be any other answer than that you were wrong about your having any real relationship with God at all, right? You're just fooling yourself!

That's exactly what Satan himself would love to be the answer you jump to. He wants you to be confused and to question your salvation. He wants you to think you are a hopeless sinner destined to hell no matter what you do. He will even use others, even people close to you, by tricking them into telling you that your relationship with God isn't as right as you think, and that you aren't really saved. He loves to muddle the waters!

The problem with this idea is that, if you think or believe that committing a sin suddenly snatches away any and all means of being forgiven of your sins, then you are also taking away your belief in faith in Christ that he is enough to forgive you and save you. Christ does not make conditions. He does not turn and run away from you insulted and crying like a mere human might.

The truth is that nowhere in the Bible does it state that becoming a Christian means you never sin again. Accepting Christ as your savior and putting your faith in him for forgiveness and protection simply means that, should sin arise again....should that stumbling rock of lust, greed, ill will or anything of the kind suddenly appear in your path and trip you, Jesus makes himself available at your call to pick you back up and help carry you on. Those since too shall become forgiven as long as you ask.

This does not mean that people go on sinning intentionally and living lives of pure evil or ill will and "Oh, don't worry. Jesus will clean it up for me." If you allow for this kind of attitude, just remember that this is the same as walking up to Jesus on the cross on Calvary, taking the palm of your hand, dipping it into His blood and just smearing it scornfully in His face with little care in the universe as to the consequences. Does not sound very delightful, does it? Should this happen, I'm quite sure that, in the words of Jesus, "it would have been better if you had never been born at all" than to face what will await you.

Some of the days I face go quite smoothly. I don't feel bad about anything. No thoughts of lust or anything else bad drift through my mind. I find myself speaking only pleasantly or at least with a normal attitude. Then, a lot of days come along where thoughts of ungodly desires tempt me. Sometimes I fall for them by overthinking on them or acting on them. Sometimes I know to turn to God right away and not allow myself to fall. But, if I do fall, I know that, before the end of the day, I have my savior Jesus to turn to for forgiveness. I confess those sins to him daily, and I ask him to forgive me and provide me with even more strength to face them.

God tells us in the Bible, in his own Word, that some battles we will win, and some battles we will lose. For the ones we do lose, we should not worry about losing our salvation, but rather turn those into a lesson to learn for the future. Do what God loves to do, take a bad situation and instead turn it into something great.

When I was very small, for some strange reason I found myself fascinated with fire. I loved a good campfire, a roaring fire in a fireplace or even the burning of coals in the grill. I guess this fascination might be explained by my associating the fire with something pleasant, like roasting marshmallows and wieners over the campfire and in the fireplace, or the sizzling hamburger patties or steaks my dad cooked on the grill on the spring and summer weekends. Or, perhaps I just liked the beauty of the flames. I certainly never wanted anything bad to happen with fire, but I enjoyed lighting matches and just burning a leaf, for example. Just watch it burn out and then move on with my day.

My parents normally kept a large box of matches on one of the shelves in the kitchen pantry. Whenever I felt like playing with one, I'd slip into the kitchen when no one was about, reach into the pantry and slide a match out, pocket it and leave out the back door. I never went down into the woods to light them. Instead, I always stayed somewhere near the edge of the yard yet hidden from sight, such as the backside of the large playhouse my dad built for my sister behind our main house. From there, I'd find a dried leaf and light it and just enjoy.

My parents and even my grandparents knew if my fascination in playing with fire. For that reason, I always had supervision whenever sitting next to a campfire or a grille. I was told numerous times not to play with the fire or matches, but being under ten years of age and a stubborn child, I blew off their worries as I knew I'd never do anything bad like start a forest fire or light up a house. I knew better, or so I believed.

On the day of the incident that I am about to reveal here, I for some reason decided instead of hiding behind the playhouse to instead go to the side of our house facing away from our nosy neighbor. Surely, all anyone from our house need to do was round the corner and I'd surely be caught, so I don't remember why I chose this spot. One of my mom's bushes that only bloomed in late spring and early summer sat dormant at the time, which I believe was late fall, and its bushy blooms had turned dried and dead. Each branch of the bush resembles a large brown Q-tip with its outside end covered in the dead blooms. I thought, what an excellent torch this might make, which might be what drew my attention to that area instead of my usual hiding place. So, using the match I'd already smuggled from the kitchen pantry earlier that morning, I lit the end of one of those branches.

Unfortunately, I had not removed the branch far enough away from the bush before part of those dried blooms fell quickly off the end and into the rest of the bush. From there, the entire side of the bush roared into flames.

The fear of the house catching on fire next quickly vacated my brain of any worries a out getting in trouble for playing with matches. I hurried to the front door of the house and yelled to anyone listening that a bush was on fire. My dad and brother quickly came out, and the garden hose was turned on and dragged around to the side of the house where the flaming bush received the proper extinguishing. Luckily, only a portion of the bush burned, and the wall of the house appeared untouched.

I received the roaring of a lifetime from my dad who followed me into the house screaming about how careless, crazy and dangerous my act of setting that fire, and playing with matches in the first place, had been. I wound up in my bedroom sitting on the edge of my bed and sulking, the tears streaming. How could anyone forgive me for something so stupid? After all, I knew better, didn't I?

I heard my dad and brother talking about the situation, and the voices became calmer. After a few minutes, my dad came into my room. He sat down next to me on the bed. In a calm voice, he explained again how dangerous a result the stunt I pulled might have come to if the fire had been worse. But, he then calmly explained that he forgave me. The fear I experienced was punishment enough and he felt just that alone probably taught me never again to play with matches the rest of my life.

Was he correct? Absolutely. My panic over almost setting the house on fire and endangering my family took a massive toll on me. I never again touched a match without permission or lit anything with a match or lighter until I was older, probably in my teen years, and then it was only to assist my parents by lighting our barbecue grill, turning on the space heater or something else chore-related.

The experience made me think of our father God and his forgiveness through Christ Jesus. The sins we commit in our lifetimes range from not-so-bad-if-you-think-about-it to the most evil and vile actions we might possibly commit. All of us have at least committed one or more sin that mere humans consider minor, such as lust in the heart or deceit. But, to God, a sin is a sin and does not have a "level" to it. All sin is equally bad in his eyes. However, no sin is bad enough not to be forgiven if we place our trust in Christ to help receive that forgiveness.

Just as my dad forgave me for the flaming bush and did not lose an ounce of the love he always gave to me, so does God forgive us when we trust in Christ. When we do stumble and ask for that forgiveness, God does not snatch away any of that love he holds for us nor do we lose an ounce of the salvation provided by Christ. So long as our faith in Him remains strong, so does the forgiveness He promises.

So when you stumble, don't fear that Jesus won't forgive you this time or the next time. Don't be afraid that salvation is lost, and don't let anyone make you feel afraid. Jesus never leaves your side as long as you reach out to Him. You know your savior, and you know His love remains true. I know he remains by my side steadfast, continuously working on me from day to day and helping me to grow in my faith and my relationship with God. No matter how many temptation stones get tossed in my path causing me to stumble, I continue to let Christ lift me and carry me through on the uphill climb to the final victory.

Therefore do not worry about tomorrow, for tomorrow will worry about itself. Each day has enough trouble of its own.

Matthey 6:34

In my early twenties while attending college and working at same, I finally took the huge life-step of moving out of my parents' house and into my very own apartment. For the first time in my life, I was going to be on my own and taking care of myself. A little part of me felt anxiety of living alone for the first time, but the majority of my felt such elation at the idea of being able to do what I wanted without worrying about anyone else in the house with me.

The apartment, located just south of downtown Birmingham, consisted of one bedroom and one full bathroom with a living room, dining area, kitchen and even a separate office area with a privacy partition that could have been used as a second bedroom. Being a writer, it made the perfect location for my office as it faced the sliding glass door leading out onto the balcony and provided a lovely view of Red Mountain in the distance. The whole apartment made the perfect first bachelor pad.

The financial aid that I received for my schooling normally issued payment at the beginning of every college term provided I signed up for classes. They paid the school directly for those classes. Afterward, there was always left an extra bit of money after classes and books were paid for. That extra in turn got sent to me through electronic deposit. I wisely put this extra money toward paying my bills and rent. The leftover amount always worked out to assist me with bills and rent for the remainder of the school term until the next.

Once I graduated school and went to work full-time at my first professional job, I no longer had financial aid to fall back on. The money I made from my first real job, this one as a branch representative for a local bank, managed to cover me for my bills and rent, but it left very little for groceries and gas. I found myself applying for credit cards and then using these to help me get by with monthly extras and necessities. As most young people in their twenties often do, I found myself sinking into the quicksand of debt. My student loan payback payments started up just a few months after graduation. During this time, I'd also made my first ever purchase of a car directly from a dealership instead of a used seller, so car payments also factored into my monthly budget. A recession occurred and gas prices skyrocketed as did the cost of groceries, adding even more to my spending budget. So, the cards began to rack up charges and, in turn, lots of interest.

Before I new it, the payments just for the credit cards alone began drowning me. It came a time where the spending became so great that I found myself one evening sitting on my bed and questioning my future. The very next day, I had a credit card payment due. I had no groceries in my pantry, and just enough money sitting in my bank account to either get those groceries or make that credit card payment, but not both.

I realized the position I now found myself in, all of which I had only myself to blame. Had I not gotten started on charging the cards, perhaps God might have provided another way. Why didn't I go to Him in the beginning instead of choosing to follow the worldly path of the "norm" which was "just get yourself a credit card to help you out." It seemed to simple a decision yet so foolish in the end.

Filing for bankruptcy or consolidation seemed a terrifying decision to make. After all, I still rented an apartment and possessed a car with a lien still on it. If I made the decision of getting financial assistance, how would this effect my credit score and my chances of purchasing a house in the future? I once again found myself stumbling onto the path of the "norm" where humans seek out what the world normally does to resolve a situation rather than asking the heavenly Father for guidance.

No, this time I refused to allow myself to be fooled into entering that path again!

That evening as I sat on my bed, I prayed to God regarding my situation. I asked him for guidance and to lay his answer on my heart. As I did, the feeling of peace crept further and further into my heart. I felt myself becoming relieved. I began thinking that a payment for a credit card certainly would not put food on my table tomorrow, and I had to eat. So far, I'd made good on those payments. Tomorrow, refusing to pay it would not immediately land me in a pit of fire. What I needed to do was call the credit card company. If they refused to help, then God assured my heart that He'd help me find further assistance.

Why didn't I just seek help from my family, you might ask? Because I knew that, as I suffered through my own financial crisis, my parents were facing their own money challenges, and so was my sister. My brother had little to no money to his name. Asking any of them for assistance was out. Besides, I'd made a solemn promise to myself before I ever left home that, once I moved out, I'd never ask my parents for a single cent. They'd spent my whole childhood caring for me and seeing to my needs. I wasn't about to attempt to burden them again once I found myself grown and on my own.

After my prayers that night, I went to sleep quite relieved. I woke up the next morning with the confidence and assurance that I at least had a plan, thanks to my Father in Heaven. The memory of a verse I'd heard from church in years past, words that Jesus shared to his disciples, now haunted my mind:

Therefore do not worry about tomorrow, for tomorrow will worry about itself. Each day has enough trouble of its own.

I remembered how he told them to look at the birds in the air and the flowers in the field, and notice how they worry not about what they might eat or what clothes they might wear. I felt humbled in the reminder. There I was on my bed the night before while tears dripped down my face and I wondered how I would survive. Why didn't I remember my own faith? I should know better than to worry about this.

I made the calls and started the process of no longer worrying. Of course, the credit card companies were of no help, but I expected nothing more when I called. However, I was successful in getting consolidation to help with the handling of my credit. From there, I began planning on how to better myself on handling my finances. I even went so far as to take a short class on managing funds from month to month, paycheck to paycheck.

It took a few years, but eventually my credit came back on track. The credit cards were paid, and I got rid of all but one (the one I kept only to make sure my credit score history continued). Very soon, my debt became very slim. I even paid off my car and received my title. With the money I had left over from my paychecks that no longer went to paying on credit cards and car payments, I made deposits into my savings account which began to rapidly grow. I then continued to pray to God for the next step, and the next step, and so on.

I look back now and see how God pulled me up from my financial constraints. He gave me the wisdom to make the wisest decisions and the strength not to let my fear get in the way. In recent years, I have been financially secure and know that I never needed to worry about things like "credit scores." God has control over all things if we allow Him.

Even now as our country faces another recession, and my retirement investment takes a hit causing me to worry, I look back on this lesson learned. I know I need not worry about what the future will bring. Instead, I turn toward my faith in God and relax in his arms of protection and guidance. In my heart and mind, I know He take care of me. So, there is no need to worry about tomorrow, what I will eat and what I will wear. God has this, and He will provide!

"I tell you the truth, Jesus said, "this poor widow has given more than all the rest of them."

Luke 21:3

"If you didn't give it to your church, then it's no longer a tithe," the head of the deacons told me one Sunday morning on the way into Sunday School.

While writing the last chapter about my financial crisis and what I learned about faith in that matter, I found myself reminded of another lesson about finances I learned and felt very strongly that I needed to share here in this chapter. That matter is the act of tithing, or giving.

That Sunday morning on the way into Sunday school, I felt so happy going into church because of a decision that God placed in my heart that week about my giving. I'd just received my paycheck electronically deposited that Friday. My normal practice on payday weekends was and still is to make sure to give an appropriate portion of my paycheck to my church as a tithe. For those who do not know what a tithe is, the regular definition per the Webster dictionary is "one tenth of annual produce or earnings, formerly taken as a tax for the support of the Church and clergy." The term actually comes from the old testament and God's command to bring one-tenth of earnings into "the store house", which people over the years presumed meant the church or place of worship so that it might always be supplied with food and other needs.

While listening to the radio on my way home after work that evening, I heard one of the local stations broadcasting a telethon of music while advertising for a charity even that week for the local Children's Hospital. The purpose of the charity was to bring in donations of funds to go toward the research of cancer in children and perhaps even move closer to finding a cure. I've always loved children and spent nine years as a teacher in my church in the children's and youth department. Certainly, this charity tugged at my heartstrings.

Something else entered my heart. I felt a pull there much like the one I felt when I was a child and decided to become a Christian. My tithe came to mind with this pull of the heartstrings. Instead of giving that money to the church like you normally do, I heard a voice saying as it whispered to my heart, why not instead give it to this charity just this one time? You can continue to give to the church starting with the next.

But isn't tithe meant only for the church, I asked myself. As usual, the skepticism of my human side reared its irritating head in a matter where it normally causes nothing but doubt.

I thankfully chose a better route to deal with the skeptic thoughts that arrived in this matter: I went straight into prayer. It took little to no time for God to push me once again in answer. In fact, no other answer presented itself but one: I needed to donate my giving to this charity. God saw it as just enough to help add to their cause.

When I went to church that Sunday morning, and the teacher who happened to be the head of ushers walked in, I told him about my happiness. I'd felt so elated all weekend long about my connection with God and His using me in my giving me. I never meant to brag, mind you. I only wanted to share my happiness and made sure to give God the glory in it.

Rather than the smile and encouragement I expected, I instead received a frown and the fast response, "Then it's no longer a tithe. It can't be a tithe unless you give it to the church! So, you still owe a tithe regardless."

Something about these words stung my very soul. Anyone with common sense alone who heard this response would say that, surely, this is wrong. It sounds so selfish and greedy, and anyone who truly knows God is neither of those things, at least in the wrong sense. He's greedy for our souls and our faith, but certainly not for our money.

I then remembered something to this effect in the Bible as far as giving and what it means. In Matthew 25:42, Jesus's words are "I tell you the truth, when you did it to one of the lest of these my brothers and sisters, you were doing it to me." Does that not mean that when we give unto those less fortunate, including research to help ill children, we are doing this for God and unto God as well. It sounds that way to me.

As for bringing the tithe to the storehouse, Jesus also said in Matthew 6: 19-20, "Do not gather together for yourself riches of this earth. They will be eaten by bugs and become rusted. Men can break in and steal them. Gather together riches in heaven where they will not be eaten by bugs or become rusted. Men cannot break in and steal them." I fully believe that anytime we give unto someone less fortune or to aide someone in any way, we are doing the same for God and unto God. We are bringing out giving to store up in heaven with God, not to store in some brick and mortar building.

Does this mean we don't have to give anything to our church? In no way do I mean to imply that here. By all means, we should give to our church to support its leaders and help with church finances and to provide food the church can give to the hungry. Most importantly, we should give to our church to help our outreach to grown among the nations. In order to have missions and send missionaries, money is unfortunately required, so by all means give to the church and give to our missions.

What I am saying is that when God lays it on a followers heart to for one time or a few times give that tithe or offering to another outlet that God knows is in dire need of it at that time, no man or woman should ever tell that follower, "Well then you didn't truly give it to God and you still owe your church. The church is not the building, it is the body of Christ and the followers who make up that body. And, whenever you do unto the least of them, you absolutely do unto Him!

Another problem I once ran into with a problem caused in a church regarding tithe occurred in my teen years at a church we joined during my middle-school years. The church we went to included some of the more prominent, or at least liked to think they were prominent, members of the surrounding communities to tended to tend from their massive incomes so that the church spent money on electronical equipment and technology of the highest caliber for use in its service, easter pageants and Sunday School classes.

The pastor of this church prided himself on making sure to make the last Sunday of the first month of the year the special Sunday where he always held his sermons regarding tithing. He made it a point to declare that anyone who did not tithe at all, or tithed but only a certain amount less than the ten percent required in the old testament, were by all means thieves robbing God from his rightful money. One year, he even went a step further by holding up a folded piece of paper in his hand and waiving it about over the congregation from his pulpit. He said, "In my hand is a list of the bad, more bad and worst tithers in this congregation. If you people do not better yourselves in your tithing, I will read this list aloud during a future worship service to shame you!"

As we drove home from that particular "bad, more bad and worst tithers list" sermon, my mom seethed with rage. "Who does he think he is," she asked. "He's really keeping tabs on how much each person gives? How does he know what their income is? And how is it any of his business? How much a person tithes is between that person and God and has nothing to do with the pastor or anyone else in the church!"

Her words prove right. The Bible speaks elegantly on this matter in the New Testament in the book of 2 Corinthians 9:6-8, "Each of you should give what you have decided in your heart to give, not reluctantly or under compulsion, for God loves a cheerful giver. And God is able to bless you abundantly so that in all things at all times, having all that you need, you will abound in every good work."

The Bible acts as sort of a "blue print" for salvation if one looks deep enough at it. At least, this is what I've been taught in my adult years on understanding the Word. The Old Testaments shows man's struggle with sin, his constant sin and his need for a savior as well as the prophecies of the coming of said savior. The New Testament then introduces that savior, Christ Jesus, who sacrifices himself to cleanse us of our sins and tear down the veil between us and God. With Jesus, we now have a way to a solid relationship with God. Sacrifices like people of the old testament put into practice, such as slaughtering an animal or something of the like, are no longer required as Jesus presented himself as the FINAL sacrifice.

Tithing in the Old Testament is described as a sacrifice. It was just one of many sacrifices required for satisfying God, asking for forgiveness, showing faithfulness and so forth. Because Christ was the final sacrifice, it seems to me that tithing and giving should no longer be considered a sacrifice any longer is it was before, but something we now do freely and happily. As for the amount we give, that remains between the individual giver and God.

I see nowhere in the Bible where any authority comes bestowed on the church or pastor on how much a congregation member gives and where he or she gives it. Anytime a church becomes a money-driven church, it's time for that church body to stop and assess its relationship with God. Money should never come before God. A church, just the same as an individual, should have faith in God to protect and provide for it.

Pastors have no business knowing how much each and every family or individual gives to the church fund. If he finds his church in need of money, then go to God and pray for it. Do not place accusations on your congregation that are not biblically founded. The next time you do feel the need to cast judgement, please take a long look in your mirror. The Bible also warns about such foolishness as judgement, and I will proceed on to that in the next chapter.

As for my giving of my tithe (yes, it was still a tithe no matter what anyone else believes), I felt God place the confidence on my heart that I made the right decision, and He held no judgement against me at all in following His request. The next time I tithed, it went to the church, but never again did I question any time where I felt God on my heart instruction me occasionally if he needed my giving to go elsewhere temporarily. As the old adage goes, "God works in mysterious ways," and indeed He does, even with our giving. Trust in Him that He will take your giving and work his Will with it. And by all means, continue to give cheerfully. Don't let anyone every make you feel wrong in how you do it as long as you feel God's pull in that right direction. Only you and you alone know what He wants from you individually, and only He and He alone will guide you correctly.

Judge not lest ye be judged. For with what judgement ye judge, ye shall be judged, and with what measure ye mete, it shell be measured to you again.

Matthew 7:1-2

The boy only wanted to belong with kids his own age and a crowd where he no longer found himself on rock bottom. My sister first found out about him through a friend at work. He was the son of said coworker and recently sought help with a drug problem. He used to drink heavily with his pals on the weekends, unbeknownst to his parents and those of the so-called friends of his. They smoked pot and live promiscuous lives with their girlfriends.

Instead of using his real name, I will call this boy Joshua for the purpose of this chapter.

The day came that he realized his life now spiraled out of control, and if he failed to do something right away, he might enter a dark path from which he might never return. Instead, he chose the better path and got away from the drugs. He wanted to hang out with new friends. A better crowd who would support his decision for a healthier lifestyle. He also quit drinking.

My sister spoke to Joshua and encouraged him to come and spend time with the youth group at our church (for purposes of what happens later in this story, I want to point out that this church happens to be the same one we attended where the tithe-obsessed minister I spoke of in the previous chapter threatened to read the list of worst tithers. At the time, we were still attending there) and make friends. On a few of the afternoons during the week and even on Saturday, some of the teenage boys in our church enjoyed using the church's gymnasium to play basketball and fellowship with each other. At the time, we had a good group of boys who my sister felt would be a great influence on this young man. She told Joshua that perhaps they might make the best support group to support him in straightening out his life. He happily followed her suggestion and, the following week, came to the church where he met the boys and began playing basketball with them. A month went by, and Joshua now began attending the Sunday School classes for the youth boys. He found himself reading the Bible more often and studying the scriptures closer than before. Joshua wanted to grow closer to God and seek salvation.

The time came where he spoke to our youth minister who led the youth department of our church at the time this happened. I'll call the minister Dusty here. He spoke to Dust and asked about how to become a member of the church and join the youth group full time. Now, one might expect in this type of situation that a caring youth minister upon hearing such a request would respond by such means as praying with the boy, talking to him about his decision and making sure he understands the Gospel of Christ and how to grow in his relationship with God.

The youth director instead spoke to him about an "agreement" that the youth department at that church at the time this happened required their students to sign when becoming a youth member. Never have I heard of any other church doing this. So long as a youth's parents are bonified members of the church, then said youth also becomes considered a member. But, Dusty decided to do take it upon himself to do this agreement for the youth department. That agreement was a cardboard page that stated something like the following:

1) *I have not and will not ever participate in drugs or alcohol.*
2) *I have not and will not participate in premarital sex.*

Dusty passed these out in the existing youth department when he became minister, requiring all of the students to sign and date it. He also made sure to provide one to every new member who came along after the fact. This went to both the boys and the girls. This agreement seems pretty extreme for a youth director to be passed out in church. I assume he felt that this might help teach the students responsibility over their bodies and decisions in middle school and high school. Keep in mind too that the pastor of our church gave his permission to Dusty to extend these to our youth.

When Joshua read the card and the two commitments provided, he knew right away that signing this agreement meant lying. He'd already has experience dabbling in drugs and alcohol, and he'd already engaged in premarital sex. The point was that he made the decision to turn from this lifestyle and start anew in Christ. He went to dusty and explained the situation to him.

You might think that Dusty, being knowledgeable about Christ, the gospel and the Bible as a whole, might respond with something along the lines of, "Well, that is understandable. You committed what the Bible described as sin, but you are now repenting and choosing Christ as your savior for faith and for forgiveness. You are asking forgiveness, and as Christ extends it, so should we." You'd think this was the response, yes?

No. To our horror and rage, he instead responded with, "Well, if you can't sign this agreement, then you can't be a part of our youth group."

This response took Joshua by complete surprise. "But look," he replied, "I'm not going to be doing those things anymore. I'm working very hard on changing my life and just want to come to know Jesus more."

"I'm sorry," said Dusty, "but you still can't join our group unless you are able to sign the agreement."

Joshua felt judgement and rejection as any person in this situation might. Because of being turned away from the group, he decided not to come back to church. In fact, his opinion of Christianity changed for the worse from that point. And how else could he feel going by the treatment he received from a man who claimed himself to be a follower of Christ. Would Christ have rejected Joshua in such a way? Of course not!

This incident made me think of the woman in the book of John, chapter eight, in the New Testament of the Bible. Jesus returned from the Mount of Olives to the temple to find a large crowd gathered. A group of men surrounded a woman who lay in terror on the ground. The men held stones in their hands, ready to cast them at the woman and beat her to death for her crime. When Jesus asked what she'd done to deserve such a punishment, the men responded that they caught her in the act of adultery, a great sin.

Did Jesus pick up a stone and join them? The idea never entered his thinking. Instead, he stood between the woman and the men. He bent down and began writing in the sand. Many Biblical scholars believe the words he wrote in the sand, though they appeared as gibberish to the rest of the crowd, appeared to each man with a stone as his own sin. The theory seems correct as each man dropped his stone, turned away in shame and quickly exited the scene. When none of the men remained, Christ turned to the woman and asked her who was left to judge her. No one, of course. So, Jesus responded to her, "Neither do I. Go and sin no more."

If Jesus is willing to forgive, why can't we?

When my sister heard about the incident, she called up Dusty and gave every piece of her mind to him that she could conjure up. She demanded to know why he thought turning a kid who is in such desperate need of ministering too away instead of welcoming him with open arms was such a good idea, at least in his mind? The youth minister could only respond that he did not want such a bad influence around his kids. He was afraid that Joshua's past habits my influence the rest of the youth. She questioned him about Jesus and forgiveness, but he refused to budge on his response.

After the conversation, she immediately reached out to Joshua who, as one might expect, felt total rejection. He asked her to just forget about it and that he did not want to be associated with such judgmental people anyway. He'd find his own way, he assured her.

Many times, I've heard about churches who turn people away or cast judgement. Even in one of the churches local to my area found themselves in the city's newspaper for a disturbing account. One of the choir members, a young girl in her early twenties, became pregnant out of wedlock. Instead of helping this young girl, the choir scorned her, and the director kicked her out. Even most of the other church members rejected her for her decision.

Is this being Christlike?

I hear these stories, and I can't help but bring myself back to the woman in the book of John who Jesus saved from the stoning. He did not cast her away. He did not frown on her and scold her. Instead, he forgave her. He welcomed her and showed her there is a way to be forgiven and walk a better path in life. If we are to be like Christ in anyway, then we should not be holding judgement over anyone's head for past sins, especially when that person we are holding it over is seeking out Christ for forgiveness and change.

Anytime someone is seeking Christ and comes to one of us followers for help, that person should never be turned away. They should never be prevented from joining a group of Christ followers who can help them by praying for and inspiring them. To do so is the same as preventing someone from coming to Christ at all. "Suffer the children to me, and do not hinder them, for the kingdom of God belongs to such as these," Jesus said to His own disciples when they attempted to stop a group of children from visiting with Jesus. Why should we not obey Him now in this same command.

After we left the church where Dusty led the Youth Department, a few years passed by, and he finally left his position there. I do hope the group found a new minister to better lead them in the proper way of following Christ and not acting like some sort of cult or club that required a signed form to join. I pray that Dusty learned from his error and became a better leader since. I can only pray this for him as I have not seen or heard of him since those days. But, like a lot of negative instances such as this that I have witnesses along the way of my life, I used it as a positive learning experience.

The takeaway for me was that we are not in a position to judge others for their sins, especially since we ourselves our sinners too. Through Jesus, we received grace and mercy from God that we do not deserve. Though we walked in a valley of sin, He provided us a way to receive his favor. Just the same, He can and will provide that way for others, no matter how bad they might seem in your eyes. They can receive forgiveness just as much as you if they seek out Christ. None of us came to him with already-perfect records, though we might think of ourselves in that way. He knows, and deep down so do we, that we are all sinners and no better than any other human. But, we are all equal in His eyes and loved the same by Him.

I look around at today's society and find more and more people who have left the church. When I've met some of these people and carried on conversations, and I've asked what caused them to leave, it almost always comes back to a reason to do with judgements. Many of them say they did not feel welcome because of some wrong decision they made in their past. Even though they wanted to change their ways or make their lives better, they still felt turned away by the church. To this, I can only say to my fellow brothers and sisters in Christianity that we need to wake up! We need to wake up from the stubborn judgmental blinders that we find ourselves falling behind, allow God to remove those blinders from our sight and start helping those in need. We need to reach out and see to their needs of prayer, learning and anything else we know we should be doing as the leaders that God made us to be. For if we do not, we may find ourselves under the worst judgment of all.....that of God. For no matter how "holy" you might think yourself, that judgment exempts no one who falls outside of Christ and/or His commands.

So, let's not shun them, brothers and sisters. Let us welcome them just as Jesus welcomed His own children. By this, I do not in any way mean we should condone sin, but if someone makes it clear they are seeking change and escape from their sin, then why shouldn't we help them when asked? Let's stop running people away from our church. Instead, let's reach out our vines, and let's grow!

**For even the son of man did
not come to be serve, but to
serve, and to give his life as a
ransom for many.**

Matthew 20:28

Writing the last chapter made me think about humbleness. In order to reach out our vines to others and grow in Christ, we need humbleness. Now, how does humbleness apply exactly to serving Christ? It means we need to put aside our own agendas and biases and focus on the needs of others. We need to step down from our high horse, to use an old adage, and down to the ground with everyone else, and we need to show God's glory and mercy by helping them. In the last chapter, I wrote about young Joshua who was refused entry into a youth group because of his past mistakes. Because of this, an opportunity to minister to and help a soul in need was blown. A very bad mistake. It seems to me that the youth director discussed let his own biases and agendas get in the way, blinding him in a spiritual sense to an opportunity right before his eyes.

Many things blind us from fully serving God to our capacities. Fear lies at the top of the list of blocks for many people, myself included. I remember many times in my own life during my adult years when the idea crept into my mind that I was fooling myself if I thought I was really saved. I mentioned earlier in this book about how Satan loves to plant that seed in your mind and watch it grow as your human fear feeds it. This also serves as a block in serving God because it makes you feel unworthy to serve and therefore you toss in your flag of defeat and swim in your depression. Oh, does Satan love to see this. When you find yourself feeling like this, just picture Satan sitting on the side laughing at you, and think to yourself, "Do I really want to let this fool get away with it?" Then, look to God and ask for his help in pulling you out.

Because of my worries with the sins that I've stumbled over during the course of my life, I came across many times, even in recent years, where I began questioning myself and my salvation. For nine straight years, I taught both in the children's and youth departments of the churches I attended starting in my mid-twenties. When I published my first book, I resigned from teaching only to focus on the spiritual gift of writing that God blessed me with. I felt strongly in my heart that He gave me the talent and desire to write for a reason: to use it as a vessel to reach others. So, I found myself planting little tidbits of God, good vs evil and the Gospel itself around in most of the books and stories I wrote. There was even a short while that I used my writing talents to reach out to men in prison and attempt to minister to them and offer a prayer outreach. If any avenue to do with my gift came along, I attempted to use it so long as I felt in my heart and from my prayers that God was leading me to do it.

But, even through all that, the feeling of unworthiness kept creeping back into my mind from time to time. It should have been quite obvious to me that God was working through me, but still I kept feeling doubt in my salvation. Thoughts of lust floated through my mind. Selfishness reared its head every once in a while. I listed to come pastors say "If you are experiencing this, then you don't have a real relationship with God after all," which I should have known were really the words of the devil himself coming through them. But, still I kept doubting. I prayed to God again for forgiveness and salvation.

In each and every one of these times, God spoke back to my heart. He reminded me that, though I am saved, this does not mean I will never sin again. Stumbling block still present themselves. Even the Bible tells us that there are battles that will show up in our lives, and some we will win, and some we will lose. The true fight though is to keep our faith in God alive even when we lose some battles. I began to realize then that questioning the forgiveness of God to my sins was like questioning my salvation as a whole. Not only was I doubting that Christ was enough, but I was putting myself before others in my thinking.

Instead of worrying about myself, especially since I knew in my heart I was already saved, perhaps I needed to focus that energy more on continuing to serve God in any ways He might show me in my daily life.

Another trap besides fear that many people fall into is thinking that good deeds save you. That statement lies very far from the truth. Good deeds do not save you, at least not alone. Only trust in Christ as your savior provides the salvation you need for eternal life. But, as the scripture tells us in the book of James, Chapter 2, just as good deeds without faith is dead, faith without good deeds is dead. In order to move forward in your faith and share God's glory and love with others, you must do those good deeds. The faith and the good deeds go hand in hand.

Christ presented himself as a major example of this. In one instance during the time before His arrest and eventual crucifixion, while spending time with his disciples, Christ took up a bowl and cloth in his hands. He then proceeded to kneel before his followers.....and washed their feet. It might seem a simple task and nothing more to some people, but to those of us who know Him and know God, this was probably the most amazing act of love and teaching that ever crossed our planet Earth! The son of the one who created us actually knelt down and washed the feet of mere men. The one who we as lowly humans are so unworthy of in turn lowered himself and performed the work of a mere household servant.

If Christ did this, certainly so should we. No one is above anyone else as far as humanity goes. No matter how rich or poor you are, what your place in society is or so forth, nothing makes you too good to step down and serve others in the name of God. This includes helping with outreach projects in your community, perhaps giving to a homeless shelter or just helping an elderly neighbor in need.

I once heard a friend say, "You know, I don't always need presents for my birthday or Christmas. Something as small as a card makes me smile. Even the little things make me happy." I feel like God works in the same way. No good deed is too small to make Him happy. So, when you feel you aren't doing enough for Him, or if someone else unfortunately tries to make you feel that way, remember that no good work for someone else ever proves too little for God. As I mentioned in an earlier chapter, God Himself said, "Whenever you've done unto even the least of these, you've done unto me."

Even giving to your church helps others in need. The church I belong to provides many different avenues to give to. One avenue is of course giving to the church funds that go toward salaries of the staff, food for the kitchen cupboards, supplies for the classrooms, and etcetera. The second option, probably my favorite, provides your giving to global missions. This serves to provide for our missionaries at home and abroad, giving them finances for food, supplies including anything medical for the people group they serve, and so forth. Another option gives funding to our family services in our church. This fund exists to provide for families less fortunate who fall on hard times due to unemployment, severe medical bills for a sick family member or other similar types of hardships. What wonderful avenues we have that help us to give to, and in turn help serve, so many people!

Another way we minister to others seems so simple that many people may not know it even makes a difference in serving others for God. Living our lives as best as possible for God certainly makes a difference. Other people in the world see how we live, the decisions we make and the faith we show in God to help us. They see us lean on Him during our hard times and place our trust in Him to see us through. They see this, and in turn it sets an example for them just how powerfully God's mercy, love, forgiveness and glory impacts our lives. Even by showing love to these people, concern for their well-being and prayer for their needs sets such an amazing example of how much God loves them through us.

The point is that if we ask God for opportunities to help others, and we open our eyes wide enough to keep a look out, He will reveal opportunities around us. It's up to us to take the blinders off to allow Him to show us. It's up to us to say no to the fear and yell "Get behind me, Satan!" when it tries to hinder us.

When Jesus walked the earth and aided those in need of healing, feeding or just a friend to talk to, He covered every one of these means of service and many more. He didn't say "I'm too good for this" or "No thanks, I might get my clothes dirty." No one is too far beneath. As far beneath Him as we are, He still chose to serve us instead of the other way around. Let us always follow His example and be ready to serve whenever an opportunity presents itself to us. We never know but He might be behind that opportunity.

**So do not fear, for I am with
you; do not be dismayed, for
I am your God. I will strengthen
you and help you; I will uphold
you with my righteous right hand.**
Isaiah 41:10

Just about everyone in the world experiences a fear of the dark during their early childhood. The nervousness a small boy or girl experiences when the lights go out for bedtime and they lay under the covers staring at the shadows, just waiting for something hiding in the far corner of the room to jump out and pounce. The sound of a creaking door from across the house makes them jump and shake, though the source turns out to be a natural explanation. Even I, as mentioned in an earlier chapter, experienced the fear of, and nightmares about, a witch I believed hid in my closet, invisible in the day but very much ready to come out at night as soon as the lights went out.

The element of fear finds us as early as our toddler ages, and it makes frequent, even sometimes daily, appearances for the rest of our lives. As we grow and mature, most learn how to build a defense mechanism against such things as fear of the dark or the imaginary monster hiding in the closet or under the bed. Does this mean we overcome fear completely just by growing up from childhood to adulthood? Of course not. Teenagers and adults face all kinds of fears, albeit it most of them quite different from childhood fears.

What many people may not realize is just how effectively fear can prevent us from effectively serving our God.

I remember when I first got asked to help teach in the children's department in my church. At the time, I was fresh out of college and attending a different church than I do now in recent years. The children's department was small as was the church itself. The teacher in the pre-school department was a close friend of our family so she knew me quite well. Her assistant left the church due to moving away to a different city, and so she asked me if I might fill those shoes as she wanted someone trustworthy. Still, when the idea was presented to me, I immediately went into doubt and fear. Though I was in my early twenties at the time, I still felt way too immature to be any kind of Sunday School teacher, even an assistant. She pointed out quickly though that I knew my Bible and attended church for over twenty years studying in Sunday School myself. All I needed to do is help teach what I already knew, and this being a preschool class meant the material was extremely easy to handle.

Still, the age of the children meant they were very impressionable, and any words said by an adult around them were very important and had to be carefully chosen. Doubt and fear of messing up still plagued my thoughts. Not only did I have to watch what I said around them, but I also worried about what other adults might think of this grown man in the preschool department teaching kids where only women had been known to teach up until then?

When in doubt, seek out the Lord is what I learned early in my life. So, I went to Him in prayer and asked if I should choose this opportunity and take on the task of helping teach the kids. Part of me felt excited actually as I loved kids and looked forward to being able to spend time helping them. I never had a little brother or sister to care for, something I did always want as a pre-teen kid. But this way, it would be like having several little sisters and brothers, just in a spiritual sense.

God gave me quick ease of heart that this teaching and helping with the children's class was what He wanted me to do right now. He also made me realize this would lead to not only new learning opportunities for myself but also greater works to do in the church. This was just a starting point for me, and I better not miss the opportunity. As I prayed about this, I felt the fear in my thoughts being quenched like water to flames. I decided right then to let my friend know that very next Sunday that I'd teach with her.

The years passed and I advanced from teaching in the pre-school department to joining a larger church where I became a Sunday School teacher and children's worship leader. I then progressed to the youth department where I lead a drama team that performed skits and even full plays for our congregation during services. Being a writer and a lover of acting, I really enjoyed the opportunity to do this with our youth. They put on some really wonderful performances and always brought their best game each time. This also helped me to gain new relationships with other church members that last until even in recent years. Though these kids are grown up now and moving on with their lives, some of them still keep in touch with me much to my delight.

After nine years of teaching in the church, I published my first book *Thanksgiving Hen on a Chicken Shed: Stories My Grandmother Told Me*, a short story collection of humorous and tall-tale stories mu grandmother entertained me with when I was a small child myself. I wanted to share these with future generations in an attempt to keep the southern tradition of storytelling alive. The book was a small success, and it launched me on a stronger focus on my writing. I knew that my Sunday School teaching responsibilities possible might not receive the attention they deserved, so after prayers to God on how I should handle this, He gave me the peace of mind and heart to move away from my teaching responsibilities at the end of that current Sunday School year and focus my extra time on my writing as well as some new activities He brought into my life.

God provides many opportunities to us and many avenues we can take based on the spiritual gifts He blesses us with, if only we don't allow our fears of failure, being ridiculed or rejected, or any other such human worries to block us from these pursuits. Such spiritual gifts include giving, praying, teaching and even doing physical work for others. Many other ways to serve people exist as well, but it remains up to each of us individually to seek out God for knowledge of our spiritual gift and the direction He wishes us to take. If we trust Him, then He can show us just how to use those gifts as a tool for ministry and service. We all have them. We just sometimes need a little help in realizing them.

But, we should also seek Him out for help in quelching any fears and doubts thrown our way. I find myself praying to God even to not let ME cast any fears or doubts toward myself. Sometimes we frighten ourselves into running away from an opportunity and fail at being effective in serving others. Sometimes we can be our own worst enemy.

My spiritual gift is writing. I've enjoyed this talent since I was a small boy in the second grade when I wrote my first short story. It was a story about a haunted school bus in the middle of the woods. Not something that screams "Christian influence found here," but I found myself very interested in ghost stories and spooky things back then. As I matured in my years and my writing, and I learned more about the creative process of storytelling through school and other writers, I found myself realizing that writing could also be a way to serve others, even minister.

The first novel I ever wrote was called *Haunts*. The story involved a college girl in her early twenties named Marla Hollingsworth. During her childhood, she survived a car crash that unfortunately took the lives of her mother and father. Marla came out of the wreckage the only survivor. The wreck was so terrible that only a miracle could have saved her, but as Marla grew up, her anger at God for taking away her parents from her and leaving her an orphan increase the distance between her and God. Her relationship with Him became nonexistent.

Another result of the accident is that Marla now sees spirits of the dead. They seek her out to tell their stories. She also sees dark shadowy things called "the dark ones" who seem to attack her and send her fleeing from every corner. All of the spirits cause Marla to fear, and she wants them to go away. Marla eventually teams up with a paranormal group whose team leader believes in the Christian faith. He wants to help Marla with her "gift" and attempts to minister to Marla, encouraging her that this ability of hers is not a curse but rather a gift from God that can be used to help others.

As the story progresses, a battle between God and evil wages over Marla's very soul. The dark forces attempt to scare Marla, increase her fear and keep her away from helping the living, while God continues to show signs to her that she has nothing to fear. Her faith in Him is all she needs to keep them at bay.

In *Haunts*, I purposely made sure to provide the gospel hidden throughout the story. One person who read it even reacted to me with "You seem to be really promoting God with this, aren't you?" That reaction made me smile as, indeed, the promotion of God is exactly what I mostly intended with this story. These are things I'd normally be afraid to publish these days as many people reject Christian ideas, but I refused to let my fears of rejection and social media cancellation hold me back. I allowed the book to be published as is. In many of my books, if not all of them, I always try to include some glorification to God, even if subtle, so make sure He gets some sort of recognition. Even if it's just a line from a character or some sort of act of kindness, or the winning of a battle of good over evil.

Another fear that sometimes tries to take hold of my heart is worrying about how to talk to others about Christ and what wonderful things He's done in my life. The way of the world these days with so many people against Christianity, this fear becomes more fueled than ever. It's a tricky one. But, I'm always reminded about what Luke says in Chapter 12 verse 12: "The Holy Spirit will give you the words to say at the moment when you need them." As I've prayed and meditated on this over time, I find that when I just relax and let the Lord provide the words, it comes out much easier. Not everyone wants to listen. Many turn a deaf ear to it and think me crazy. But at least I let the words come out and refused to let fear keep them blocked inside. God kept the words coming and the fear silent.

Fear acts like a crippling disease in a mental sense. As time moves on, it can even spiritually turn you into an invalid. Don't let this happen! Do not allow fear to take over your life and to cripple you. Ask God for strength against it and healing from it. Let

Him guide you away from it today. As He says to us in Isaiah 41:10, "Fear not, for I am with you; be not dismayed, for I am your God; I will strengthen you, I will help you, I will uphold you with my righteous hand."

I wish that all of your were as I am. But each of you has your own gift from God; one has this gift, another has that. Now to the unmarried and the widows I say: It is good for them to stay unmarried, as I do.

1 Corinthians 7:7-8

"So, when are you going to get married? When are you going to fall in love?"

These were the questions that constantly plagued me from friends and loved ones as I endured my twenties. From left and right came exclamations of how I needed a woman in my life to be complete. How strange I was, they felt, for not having a wife or girlfriend already next to my side. Though they most likely meant no harm, their comments made me start to feel like I was less than a normal human just because I happened to be single.

Mind you, no plan of being single even existed in my mind while growing from childhood to adulthood. In fact, I always pictured being married and having children just like many kids too as they grow and mature. It seemed the regular thing to happen to men and women. In my school years, I focused all of my energy and attention to my studies. Though I had a few non-serious girlfriends, dating wasn't something I did a lot of. My shyness at that young age can take most of the blame, but the push to make good grades in school that I received from my parents and teachers kept me focused on that as my main goal.

Even in college I continued this strong focus. I knew I wanted to be a writer, but that took a lot of work and time to pursue, and, much like the entertainment field, nothing in the world of publishing comes guaranteed. I realized in the meantime that I needed a steady job in case my writing never took off. I wanted something that provided more than enough money to support myself and help my family in need, so a college degree stayed in my sights.

Once I completed college and found a job with good support, I started back into the dating pool again. A few girlfriends came and went, but for some reason I never found that serious relationship that led to anything stronger than just dating. I began to wonder what God's plan for me was. Everyone around me seemed to have better luck finding their significant other. I looked deeply at myself and tried changing things about me physically and personality-wise because I felt sure it had to be something wrong with me. But each time I sought God out for advice, I kept feeling Him giving the same answer to my heart: "Why don't you stop worrying about it. I have better things for you."

You'd think this would give me automatic peace, and it did for a time. But before long, I kept pushing myself right back into the dating pool. One heartache after another tossed me around. Every time, I came out shaking the irritating waters of, looking up to God and hearing him say once again: "What did I tell you? Stop it! Now, let me handle it?"

Of course, others around me kept pushing me by questioning what my problem was and constantly attempting to fix me up with some. Each fixer-upper ended up in some form of disaster or another. I advised them time and again what God's message to me was, so I needed to just leave well enough alone.

During my time of splashing around, and almost drowning in, the dating pool, I did try online dating services and must comment on how comical yet sad the whole process appeared to me. A company makes money off your sadness, misfortune and loneliness by promising speedy dating service and a quick link to romance if you just join them for, say, fifty dollars a month! Guaranteed you'll get a girlfriend/boyfriend in no time and find that true romance you've spent your life searching for.

What a bucketful of pasture dung!

In my experience on those sites doing the profile searches, I mostly came across women's profiles that appeared inactive for months, some of them probably not even valid accounts. No responses to any messages, but the tip-off was the "message read" alert never activated, meaning that they were no longer on the site or the profile was fake to begin with. Spent several months on one site doing constant searches. Only a handful of the profiles were active and none of them were interested in responding to me. The other 98% were not even viewing their profiles, if they were even real people to begin with. I wasted a lot of money on these sites that could have, and should have, gone to gas for my car, groceries for my cupboards or even tithe for my church.

For the profiles that appeared active and legit, a lot of the "requirements" these ladies put out there to the gentleman viewing them made it look more like you were submitting a job resume than looking to make a date. For instance, a lot of the profiles listed a "requirements" section much like you'd find on a job posting: "Must be no less then 6 feet tall; must have annual income of no less then $100K; must have dark hair; must have dark eyes; must not weigh more than 200 pounds unless muscular; must have minimum of at least four solid past relationships for experience or prior marriage can be considered in place of experience." Yes, these were actually listed out there, or postings very similar to it with wacky requirements just to illicit a response from the girl.

What is wrong with some of you people?

And yes, I am aware that many women have probably seen similar garbage posted on profiles for men like "must have this color hair or eyes" or "must be this particular body frame or weight." Indeed, the ridiculousness unfortunately exists on both sides of the gender pool.

What really cracked me up was finding this type of requirement list on the profile for a girl who listed her own measurements of being just under five feet tall, yet she required the man she sought to be no less then six feet tall. Not able to resist the temptation to spout off, I messaged her and advised that I myself stand at five feet, nine inches, and her height makes me rather tall, so requiring six feet minimum made no sense at all. Needless to say, I received no response from that, but felt satisfied when I received the notification from the site's server that she read my message. I hope I touched a nerve.

Shallowness unfortunately still runs deep in our society, which explains why many of these people with these profiles on the online single sites remain single for so long. If you remain single and you keep hold of such a list of requirements, my advice to you would be to lower your expectations at least just a little. I definitely promise you that someone being less than six feet tall does not make them any less a man outside of height. Some of the best men in the world stand less than six feet tall. Do not allow your biased requirements to cause you to miss the opportunity of finding a great guy. And men, do not let something like a small weight problem or lacking in other bodily areas cause you to miss out on a wonderful woman. The physical body does not say everything about the person himself/herself. And, I can always harken back to that scripture "Judge not lest ye be judged." While it's not wrong to have an attraction to certain types, it's not good either to exercise full blown judgement to the extreme on someone for their physical qualities.

I can safely say that some of the most beautiful women I met turned out to be the ugliest on the inside. Take caution when placing attraction and judgement strictly on looks. Also, for some strange reason, a lot of women are attracted to bad men. My guess is they see these men as a challenge. The muscle-bound jerks who yell at them, slap them and/or mistreat them mentally. No man is worth this shame and degradation, nor is any woman. Why not let God supply you instead with someone wonderfully compatible?

The few dates I successfully made from the use of internet dating sites never went anywhere. A few of the girls I went out with disappeared shortly after the first date, and nothing will convince me that they weren't just looking for a free nice meal in an expensive restaurant. The few that continued onto second and third dates went nowhere. I began to see why a lot of these women remained single. Some possessed really rotten attitudes while others just came off plain bossy.

Throughout all this, I still felt God telling my heart that I accomplished nothing but wasting my own time and that I needed nothing more than to just be still and let Him work things out in my life. Many a time in my young adult years, I prayed to Him to lead me to my soulmate so that I might be able to marry and have children. What a strong desire I possessed to someday have a child of my own to raise and love and nurture. To date, no such soulmater ever showed up in my life, and no blessings of children of my own in my life. That does not mean some special woman still might not show up in the future. But instead of dwelling on being single and making myself feel lonely, I instead look at the accomplishments in my life that come only from God and appreciate what He's given me.

I would not have been able to teach children for nine straight years had it not been for my singleness. During those years, I saw many of the children come to know Christ and participate in baptism. This never fails to cause my heart to swell, and I thank God for His achievements and for using me in any way that I might have played a part in it.

I would not have been able to complete the many books I've published, some of those which have inspired others or at least provided a laugh and cheering up when the reader needed it most. More importantly I would not have had the ability to care for my family. This in no means slams getting married and/or having children! I gladly would have done that, and will do that, were it in God's plan for me.

Many people marry in life. God has different plans for different folks. But until then, I remain happy with what He's blessed me with in life. I own a great home and a large property, I have family who cares for my well-being and friends who make me laugh. My pantries and refrigerator stay plenished with food. I never want for anything so far as necessities go.

A very frequent problem people face, even followers of God, is the desire to always want more. They find themselves never satisfied just with what they currently own. A person may own a house just the right size for him/her, just enough furniture to get by on and all the comforts a home possibly yields, but he/she always feels the need to buy more stuff for said house. Expensive paintings for the wall. More expensive bedroom furniture. A jet tub rather than a simple shower stall. Money practically thrown out on things that said person can definitely exist without but yet still feels the need to own. I've been in that position even if just for the little things like spending money on knick-knacks or collectibles I just had to possess even though that money would go more suitably toward one of my church's many available funds.

The same most definitely goes for the life of a single person. Said person becomes forced by the society around them to feel they need someone in their life, preferably a marriage, or that person deserves no right to exist in society as a normal person. That single man/woman must forever be treated as abnormal, constantly left out of church functions or community events that a married couple or family might be more suitable to enjoy.

Pretty rotten thought, isn't it? Believe it, I have seen this attitude in society, even in churches I've been a part of in the past. The singles are shuffled to the back into their own group and treated like outcasts. They sit uninvited to participate in events and find themselves watching the married folks get the VIP treatment.

"Then why don't those singles just get themselves married," some of these society members might ask. I have a better question to throw back at them: "Why not treat the single people like members of society, acceptable as they are, and invite them too to come as they are?" Didn't Christ Himself ask us to come as we are? Does He require a person to be married in order to receive saving grace? Most certainly not.

God sometimes keeps people single for specific reasons. Some remain single so that they may serve the Lord in ways such as mission field work overseas or something of the like that they might not be able to normally do if tied down to a marriage and children. Others He might keep single so that they can care for their elders in their family without also having to tend to a family of their own. There are those as well that I am sure He keeps single solely for the fact that those people may just be happier that way.

In other words, there is nothing wrong at all with a person being single. Even if I never marry, I see that not as a burden or curse. I know I will never be alone in my life as long as there is breath in my body. Christ will remain by my side always. He is enough for me that I will never even feel the loneliness, so I refuse to let it worry me. This faith in His companionship and protection makes life a lot easier for me, and I thank Him for that every day. He provides a more spectacular kind of love, support, encouragement, and forgiveness that no human being can possibly give. When we do wrong and ask forgiveness, He holds not those wrong doings over our heads the remainder of our days. He forgives and forgets those wrongdoings, and He carries us on. He never leaves us or deceives us, though sometimes we mistakenly think He does.

So, I say to my fellow Christian brothers and sisters who are single, and all other singles for that matter, and who feel alone, that you are valuable as you are. Look deep inside for the gifts God gave you and use them. Seek Him out instead as your significant other and allow Him to use you and your life. I can speak from experience to say you will not be disappointed. You are not alone! Seek Him out and He will keep you with Him forever as long as you let Him.

To the family members and friends of the singles out there, I say that you should not make these singles feel like they do not belong because they never marry. They are people, not freaks. Lift them up and instead make them feel loved no matter what. Appreciate them for who they are and support them for their choice.

To members of the churches out there, do not make your single members into outcasts. Include them in all your activities and use the talents and gifts God blessed them with to further your missions. Being single does not make them useless any more than being married makes them special. Show them that you love them the way they are just as Christ loves them as they are. For He calls us to support one another throughout our lives, and He wants us all to come as we are and worship.

Let us all love and show support for our singles today!

He will wipe every tear from their eyes. There will be no more death or mourning or crying or pain, for the old order of things has passed away.

Revelation 21:4

My mother used to tell us when we were young, "When I am gone, don't come to my grave, and don't bring me flowers, because I will not be there." Now, years later, she passed away in 2016, and each year at least once or twice visit her grave to make sure it appears taken care of and place a new flower display. I know, we obviously didn't listen well, however old traditions remain the hardest to break. For some people, the grave of a close loved one offers a place to release grief and mediate. For us, it serves as a way to remember the good times. We know she isn't there, not in spirit.

"Because when I am gone," she told us, "I will be somewhere else in a much better place." We know that now, and that helps ease the pain and tears.

My mother suffered many years with fibromyalgia that caused pain in most of her body, mainly in her back. No attempt at treatment ever quite eased the pain enough, although some made it bearable for her. On top of these ailments, she faced onset of Parkinson's disease that affected her memory and her speech. Still, through the many medications she endures, she managed to try to be the best mom for her adult children.

In her 68th year of life, mom's ailments finally overwhelmed her body causing her organs to shut down and she lost consciousness. She went into the hospital where she was admitted to ICU. The doctors asked my dad and sister into the conference room where people dread to go when a loved one is hospitalized there, for we know what that room exists for. They told us that, though they were doing everything in their power to help her, death was unpreventable in this case.

When the time came for her to pass on to the next life, we cried and faced the difficult times of mourning. We still shed a tear or two when we remember the times of yesteryear. However, we know just as she predicted that she now rests in a much better place, in the arms of God where no pain ever exists again. She now walks, dances and whatever other movements we experience in that next life with Christ, no longer trapped in a physical body of agony and sorry, but forever free to exist in total happiness.

Death owns the distinctness of being something that exists as part of everyday life yet remains one of the hardest things to deal with in life. When a loved one leaves us seemingly forever to pass on into death, it stands to perfect understanding that the living survivor(s) feel(s) what equates as a massive hole in life and heart. I personally know of anything greater than experiencing that pain as far as loss goes. It becomes extremely difficult for a mere human being to deal with. At least, that's how our hearts feel to us and what we hear our minds tell us.

The day my family and I stood around my mother's hospital bed and said goodbye as we watched her pass on, I wondered how we all, my dad especially, would deal with this from a day-to-day basis going forward. Part of me marveled at the blessing of knowing that my mother was there to welcome me into the world, and I was able to be there to say goodbye as she left it. This helped with dealing with the closure, so I can only fathom what one feels when they do not have the opportunity to say goodbye.

My mother told us many times of her regrets of not being able to make amends with her own mother. My grandmother, or Mee-Maw as she was affectionately known, passed on three years before I was born, so I never got the pleasure of knowing her in person though I know I shall meet her in spirit one day. Mee-Maw died when she was still a young middle-aged woman due to a medical mistake in the hospital where she received a simple operation. In the days prior to that, my mom argued with her over the phone about something trivial, not knowing of the pending future as the operation to come was to be simple and even a one-day thing. When Mee-Maw passed, it about killed my mother emotionally that the last words they shared were an argument and that she never had a proper goodbye or chance to take those words back. This regret stuck with her until her own dying day.

Many times, we attempted to assure my mother that Mee-Maw took no pain with her and remembered nothing now of their argument. She need not burden herself for the rest of her life with the worries of unresolved fights. Instead, she should give that burden to God and know that, where Mee-Maw was, she forgave her and forgot those fights long ago. But, mom never let go of the guilt. She still kept a piece of it with her that revealed itself from time to time.

The night before my mom collapsed suddenly and was taken to the hospital, I had, unbeknownst to me, the final phone call I'd ever have with her in life. The conversation was filled with nothing but positive words, and the last words I heard her say were "I love you. I love you. I love you," which she repeated twice for me. I said "I love you" back to her three times. God gifted me with a final moment that I can treasure and take with me always through life.

I know that as I prayed for strength in her hospital room that day, I did automatically feel a reassurance somewhere in my heart, small at first, that we'd make it through this hard time and that we'd surely not be alone in the process. As the days went own, that feeling of reassurance only grew. Even before she passed on, I placed my faith in God to help us. I prayed for him for two outcomes: that my mom come back from the illness, be healed and be with us longer, or if it was in His plan that she must leave now, please take her peacefully with no pain. God answered the second request as the doctors and hospital took very good care of my mom in that ICU. They made sure to give her enough pain medication to make her last moments comfortable. It was God's plan that this be her time to return to her heavenly home, and I knew that even if she did survive, her conditions would only grow worse and even more painful. She needed peace now away from the pain she dealt with for so long.

God answers prayers in His own way, and in such a way that His master plan remains on track. We all have a time when our life on earth must end. That future is completed unchangeable. So, we must make our decisions on whether we trust God to get us through or whether we choose to follow the world and the majority "norm" instead.

I've heard people in times of losing a loved one turn to blaming God for taking them and getting angry with Him for not allowing more time. This reaction is only human and totally understandable under the circumstances. Often in times of distress we seek someone or something to lash out at, to place the blame on and therefore try to ease the pain somewhat. One might find it easier to blame God as they do not see or hear Him physically. As we see Him as in control of the universe, it also makes blaming him for any and all wrong much easier. Believe me though, He is there, and He does hear. He knows the pain you face and wants more than anything for you to come into His arms and lay that pain on Him.

Even though questions flood our minds as to why He took said loved one(s) and why we couldn't have just one more opportunity to be with them just a little longer, we must trust Him that His plan is the one true path to follow. We may not ever understand it in life, but as long as we keep our faith alive, one day even in the eternal spirit life, we will surely know and understand. We will love Him even more for it.

For me, I understood why my mom's time needed to be at that moment. Her condition only worsened over those years in her sixties, and we knew that, healthwise, only more agony and hardship lay ahead of her. God knew this too, and long before any of us knew. In a way, he gifted everyone in the process. Not only did he eternally release my mom from her physical pain and suffering and brought her into a much better place than this world ever offered, but he took away the further burden He knew that we as her family would face in attempting to care for her. Do not get me wrong here. Had she lived on, we would have put our all into continuing to care for her with all our love included, but God desired better plans for us too, so this path was the one He always chose for us to travel. Each day, I thank Him for leading us, caring for us, strengthening us and seeing us through our hard times.

Even with such an incredible loss dealt to us, I refuse to give up on God. I know his ultimate plan for me and everyone else still carries on. When the bad things happen, many times better things await us in life just down the road if we don't give up on hope and marching on.

When you lose a loved one, don't let the grief swallow you. Yes, you'll feel it for a time. It's easy for someone to say weep not, but we do that anyway as it helps release the anguish. Please do release it. Weep out your sorrows, but don't carry it with you forever. Put your trust on God to carry you through those hard times. Weep not forever because you only waste your energy, an energy better spent continuing with living and enjoying what time you have left with the rest of your family and friends. We can remember our loved ones and still carry on. When times feel too hard, look to God and pray for His strength. Then, just relax and let Him carry you through. You'll see that in time things feel much easier.

POSTLUDE

Thank you for taking the time to read this book. I hope it brought some sort of inspiration for your or at the least a bit of a smile for your face. Since I published my first book, I planned to write at least one book that delt solely with God's inspiration to my own life and some of the toughness in life that I made it through with His grace and mercy. The purpose was always to share that with others so that they too might see the goodness in God, that faith is not useless, and that hope remains alive.

The world deals us a lot of darkness in the politics, offensiveness, scorn, selfishness, the media influence and the cries to "follow us or we will cancel you." Believe me when I say that God will never allow you to be cancelled from His ultimate plan for you provided that you keep strengthening your faith in him and don't let the world cause it to wither. Forget what they say, because in the end, none of it will matter. Only God will matter.

The devil's biggest and greatest achievement, his ultimate shield of protection, is the doubt of people in his existence. He uses that to prowl amongst us, trip us up and fertilize our doubts so that they may grow and intertwine in our hopes. Wee him out! Don't let him cause you to doubt, to feel sorry for yourself or to fester anger at the world around you. Let your love for God lift your head above it and keep your focus on Him instead.

The greatest protection you can have in this life is the protection of Christ Himself. Believe me when I say that I have relied on this protection all of my life, and though I still face the trials and hardships of life, the protection He gives has never failed me. Never have I felt alone or unshielded from the wrath of the world. Every night when I go to bed, I end my day saying a prayer to Him for His forgiveness and His undying protection. I say this not to brag about how good I am, as without Him, I am worthless. I say this because we owe God all of the glory for any and every good thing we receive in this life, the grace and mercy he bestows upon us rather than the punishment we so rightly deserve, and just to be thankful for the blessing of another day to live and breathe. He teaches us in the Bible that we get no promise for a tomorrow, but we do get the promise of his never-ending love so long as we seek Him for it.

Seek Him out today. Study his Word often. Know Him. Give Him a try. You stand to lose nothing in the process.... nothing but your sin and shame. Then, go with Him in peace and show the world the great things He does for you. Let's love each other as He loves us, and we can show the world that there exists a love which never dies.

*I am leaving you with a gift —
peace of mind and heart. And the
peace I give is a gift the world
cannot give. So don't be troubled
or afraid.*

Jesus

ABOUT THE AUTHOR

Kevin Cain grew up in Alabama enjoying the charm of southern storytelling including his own grandmother's stories that he published in his first book "Thanksgiving Hen On A Chicken Shed: Stories My Grandmother Told Me." Writing since the ripe old age of eight, Kevin continues to share his stories and carry on the tradition of southern storytelling. He still resides in Alabama in Shelby County where he lives with his cat and three lovely little ghost girls who haunt his home.

Visit him at writerkevincain.com